THE SPIRIT OF GOD IN THE OLD TESTAMENT

CENTRE FOR PENTECOSTAL THEOLOGY CLASSICS SERIES

THE SPIRIT OF GOD
IN THE OLD TESTAMENT

CENTRE FOR PENTECOSTAL THEOLOGY
CLASSICS SERIES

LLOYD R. NEVE

CPT

CPT Press
Cleveland, Tennessee

The Spirit of God in the Old Testament
Centre for Pentecostal Theology Classics Series

Published by CPT Press
900 Walker ST NE
Cleveland, TN 37311
USA
email: cptpress@pentecostaltheology.org
website: www.cptpress.com

ISBN-10: 1935931148
ISBN-13: 9781935931140

CONTENTS

Chapter 7
'Wherever the spirit would go they went': The Spirit's
Relation to Yahweh 119

SERIES PREFACE

The Centre for Pentecostal Theology Classics Series makes available to a wider audience monograph length studies from previous generations that are of special significance for Pentecostal scholarship. While the works included are not all written by Pentecostal scholars, they all address themes and issues that inform constructive Pentecostal theology and/or make special contributions to such by means of methodology or approach.

PREFACE

It is a surprising fact that no book available in the English language has ever been written on the spirit of God in the Old Testament. The only book in recent decades to deal in a comprehensive way with this immensely important subject is *Ruach, Le Souffle dans L'Ancien Testament* by Daniel Lys. This book, which appeared in 1962, was of inestimable help and encouragement to me. The spirit of God in the Old Testament had, since 1954, been my special area of research in the doctoral program at Union Theological Seminary in New York. Lys's book gave me the confidence to believe I was on the right track (1) in my attempt to isolate for special study the spirit of God texts from other *ruach* texts (with one or two exceptions, my independently compiled spirit of God text list almost exactly corresponded to his), (2) in my dating of relevant spirit of God texts which again corresponded very closely to his, and (3) in my method of examining the texts from each of the four chronological periods in order to draw conclusions regarding the concept of the spirit in each respective period. On the one hand, although the basic results of my own study were already down on paper long before I saw Lys' book, the correspondences are so close as to make necessary this disclaimer of plagiarism! On the other hand, the fact that I learned a great deal from his book is only too evident from the numerous footnoted items in this present volume.

In placing texts in their proper historical context, I have tended to follow advice given me by the faculty advisor at UTS under whom I was writing my dissertation. In the manuscript itself, he suggested, the dating of texts must be done arbitrarily lest the texts rather than the spirit of God become the main object of concern. The texts have not been dated without serious consideration, however, but the debate over the chronology and provenance of each text seldom appears in the book. Dating a text to a certain period has meant, then, that the spirit concept in that text is dated to the same period. Only where there is serious question have I argued the dating in the footnotes.

Biblical quotations are made from the Revised Standard Version. Chapter and verse references follow the Hebrew Bible. Where they differ from the RSV, chapter and verse references for the latter are given in parenthesis.

October, 1972   L.N.

ABBREVIATIONS

AB   Anchor Bible (Garden City: Doubleday)

ANET   Pritchard, James B., *Ancient near Eastern Texts Relating to the Old Testament* (Princeton, NJ: Princeton University Press, 3d edn, 1969)

ATD   Das Alte Testament Deutsch (Göttingen: Vandenhoeck & Ruprecht)

BDB   Brown, Francis, S.R. Driver, and C.A. Briggs, *A Hebrew and English Lexicon of the Old Testament: With an Appendix Containing the Biblical Aramaic: Based on the Lexicon of William Gesenius as Translated by Edward Robinson* (Oxford: Clarendon Press, 1952).

BK   Biblischer Kommentar (Neukirchen: Neukirchener Verlag)

IB   G.A. Buttrick (ed.), *The Interpreter's Bible* (New York: Abingdon-Cokesbury Press, 1951).

ICC   International Critical Commentary (Edinburgh: T & T Clark)

JBL   *Journal of Biblical Literature*

JNES   *Journal of Near Eastern Studies*

RB   *Revue Biblique*

ZAW   *Zeitschrift für die Alttestamentliche Wissenschaft*

1

INTRODUCTION

Probably nothing in the Old Testament so eludes comprehension as the spirit of God. Yet there it was, taking possession of Gideon, coming mightily on Saul, inspiring the prophets, anointing the messiah, and renewing all of creation in the new age. It made a heroic warrior out of an ordinary farm boy, a prophetess out of a slave girl. It could create from the driest desert a fertile paradise, and even more astonishing, could make obedient a stubborn, intractable heart.

When the Hebrews wanted to speak of this spirit, they called it God's *ruach* (רוּחַ). They had ready at hand this word which in an earlier Palestinian culture, the Ugaritic, had meant only wind. But how fitting a term it was to express the mystery of the spirit's activity. Wind is intangible, invisible. Just as the movement of the wind lay beyond the control of humankind, so also the coming of the spirit could only be awaited, never coerced (not even by Solomon who must have ardently wished to climax the glory of his reign with this ultimate authentication). Just as life-giving moisture was brought by the west wind, so the spirit could be the bearer of life and fertility. Just as the east wind off the desert could be harsh and punishing, so God's spirit was often filled with wrath and bitter judgment.

When Israel spoke of the *ruach* of God they were using a *concept* that was found nowhere else in the Ancient Near East. Certainly, the wind in the Mesopotamian cultures existed and functioned in the divine realm as a special instrument of the gods and in Egypt was even divinized as the god Amon-re. Yet no other nation in the Ancient Near East spoke of its gods as having a spirit. In a peculiar people with a singular Lord it was a unique concept.

What did the Old Testament writers mean when they spoke of God's *ruach?* What did they mean to express about Yahweh and his activity when they applied this term to him?

Even though they used *ruach* with this background meaning of wind, and even though the term in large part retained the connotations of movement, power, and mystery, yet in applying the term to Yahweh, they began to designate some very definite things about their God. The most obvious and most persistent aspect of his nature thus expressed by *ruach* is the power which he utilizes in relation to his creation (Isa. 31.3). But other meanings soon came to be expressed by the same word. God has life and when he bestows this life on his creation the life itself can be called *ruach* (Isa. 32.15). Israel experienced Yahweh's wrath directed against themselves or acting on their behalf against an enemy. And as they experienced the wrath of their God they could refer to it as *ruach* (Isa. 30.28). In their history as a people they could perceive Yahweh's guidance, his will for them, and this will of Yahweh, as it was directed toward his people, could be called *ruach* (Isa. 30.1). In a related meaning they thought of Yahweh as having a mind (in Hebrew, לֵב, *leb),* and this also, as it was communicated to his creation, was known as God's *ruach* (Isa. 40.13). Finally, at least three of these meanings – power, life, and anger – were expressed metaphorically as breath *(ruach).*

In the Old Testament literature *ruach* is only used to express God's activity *as he relates himself* to his world, his creation, his people. It was Israel's way of describing God, not as he is in himself, but as he communicates to the world his power, his life, his anger, his will, his very presence.

I. The Disparity of *Ruach* and Spirit

'Spirit' is the word commonly used in translating *ruach.* Because spirit, as well as *ruach,* bears the background meaning of wind with the same connotations of movement, power, and invisibility, it is the most suitable word to use as the translation of *ruach.* Furthermore, spirit as used in the phrase 'spirit of God' suggests God as active outside himself, and in this sense is also a good translation of the relational meaning of *ruach.*

It is a question, however, whether all these meanings borne by *ruach* as it was applied to God by the Hebrews can be adequately translated by the word spirit. Certainly the meanings of life, power, and Yahweh's presence, as expressed by *ruach,* are translatable by the word spirit. The meaning of *ruach* as it came to designate Yahweh's will can also be conveyed by spirit. Anger, mind, and breath, however, are not meanings called up by the English word spirit, used alone. For example, spirit can mean disposition, but for a certain kind of disposition such as anger a qualifying word must be used. Spirit cannot mean intellectual faculties. Nor can spirit be used to mean breath. For these meanings of *ruach* it is necessary to use the alternate terms anger, mind, and breath, bearing in mind, however, that for the Hebrew, any of these meanings could be expressed in relation to God by the one phrase, *ruach elohim.*

II. *Ruach's* Trifurcation of Meaning

The subject of this study is the spirit of God in the Old Testament. This means that the primary concern is not the whole of the word *ruach* and its meanings as used in the Old Testament but rather one aspect of *ruach*, *ruach* as used to refer to God and his activity, what is traditionally called 'the spirit of God'. This is not, however, the only meaning of *ruach* in the Old Testament. It retained its original meaning of wind, and in addition was used to refer to the human spirit.

It cannot, therefore, be merely a matter of isolating the passages that speak of *ruach* and investigating them. Because the subject is not *ruach,* but rather, 'the spirit of God', it will be necessary to identify the passages in the Old Testament which speak of the spirit (*ruach*) of God as distinguished from the wind (*ruach*) and the spirit (*ruach*) in the creature in order to make the proper exegetical study necessary for an understanding of the spirit of God. This means that the classification of the different meanings of *ruach* will differ from that found in the lexicons, which frequently give the separate classification of 'breath'. But human breath, obviously, is only one aspect of the total meaning of the *ruach* in humankind. And 'breath' as applied to God is only used metaphorically to indicate his spirit. Therefore the classification proposed here is not wind, breath, spirit, but rather wind, *ruach* in humanity (whether breath or spirit), and *ruach* of God.[1]

III. Origin and Development

The existence and reality of the spirit of God, as distinguished from spirits, from spirit, or from wind, is unquestioned in the later literature of the Old Testament. If then the prophets and writers of post-exilic Israel spoke and wrote of a power, a reality, a life coming from God and thought of as the spirit of God, a reality so distinct in its delineation that its coming could be anticipated even into the new age, it must next be asked, how far back into the early reaches of Old Testament literature can this concept of the spirit of God be traced? And secondly, how does the concept develop, what new meanings does it take on, what is the image that finally emerges at the end of the Old Testament period? These are the questions to be investigated in this study.

---

[1] Johannes H. Scheepers, *Die Gees van God en die Gees van die mens in die Oud Testament* (Kampen: J.H. Kok, 1960), and Daniel Lys, *Ruach, le Souffle dans l'Ancien Testament* (Paris: Presses Universitaires de France, 1962), have constructed their studies around just such a triple classification.

2

'AT THE BLAST OF THY NOSTRILS':
THE EARLIEST TEXTS

Yahweh's spirit in the earliest texts[1] is described in terms which reflect the characteristics of this period of Israel's beginnings. It was
a period of assimilation, innovation, and consolidation.

Maximum exposure to outside influences would be expected for
Israel, newly arrived in Canaan. For this reason, it is this early period particularly which provided points of contact with other cultures in its description of the spirit.

By joining in the covenant with Yahweh at Sinai, Israel introduced a new and revolutionary monotheism into the ancient Near
East. New movements, until they become 'domesticated', exhibit
elements which appear rough and violent. The spirit of God in this
period, which is anything but calm and gentle in its manifestations,
borrows heavily on these characteristics.

Along with innovation comes adjustment and consolidation.
From existence in Egypt, Israel moved to a semi-nomadic existence
in the wilderness, then to a settled existence in Canaan. Starting
with the singular leadership of Moses; Israel had to readjust to the
installation of the elders, then to the institution of the judges, and
finally to the monarchy. Many systems were attempted and each
needed the ultimate certification that was provided by Yahweh's

---

[1] Dating from Israel's earliest beginnings to the middle of the ninth century
BCE, the texts from this period are early poetry (Exod. 15.8, 10; Num. 24.2; 2
Sam. 22.16; 23.2) and early historical writings (Gen. 41.38; Num. 11.17, 25, 26,
29; Judg. 3.10; 6.34; 11.29; 13.25; 14.6, 19; 15.14; 1 Sam. 10.6, 10; 11.16; 16.13, 14;
19.20, 23).

spirit. Thus the spirit described in these texts is to an overwhelming degree the charismatic spirit.

In short, the spirit of God described in these earliest texts is very much a part of this period.

I. Assimilation

More than at any other time in her history, Israel's faith in these early days was most open to outside influences. The sojourn of certain tribes in Egypt was still a relatively recent memory. This presupposes a direct acquaintance with Egyptian culture and religion on the part of a large number of those who were instrumental in the formation of Israel's beliefs.

This was a time also when to a maximum extent the young nation's traditions were being molded, melded, and enlarged. This means that the patriarchal traditions also were being retold by each tribe to the whole nation at worship. Whatever strains from early Mesopotamian or early Canaanite cultures were hidden in these patriarchal traditions could now exert an influence on Israel's faith.

Settlement in Canaan also involved, of course, daily contact with the Canaanite way of life. This Canaanite influence is evident, for example, in Israel's earliest laws and in the inclusion of non-Israelite traditions in the patriarchal narratives of Genesis (for example, Gen. 21.15-21). Direct contact with non-Yahwist Canaanites was supplemented by the inclusion in Israel itself of many non-related tribes, for example, the Kenizzites or the Kenites (Judg. 1.11-20). Each of these tribes would contribute its own cultural background to Israel's total religious heritage.

Assimilation during this early period was not only aided by the availability of outside influences but also by Israel's readiness to accept them. Her own institutions and theology were not fixed as they were in later periods but were still in the primary stages of formation. It may even be asserted that Yahwism in its early stages had a vigor and vitality which could reach out towards, rather than draw back from, extraneous influences. It could absorb without being absorbed. The xenophobia present in certain postexilic biblical writings was not yet evident.

Assimilation was not indiscriminate, however, and actually was not as abundant as the possibilities might suggest. On the contrary,

the startling thing may be that so little of the thought world of Israel's neighbors actually penetrated Israel's theology. What examples
there are in the spirit of God texts are only loosely related to pre-
Israelite cultures or else show only the aftermath of a negative reaction. Most of the Israelite texts from this early period are actually
without parallel in the ancient Near East and exhibit no contact at
all with other religions in their concept of the spirit.

A. Divine Wind

The two texts which show the greatest contact with the divine
wind[2] concept that existed in neighboring cultures are Exod. 15.8,
10 and 2 Sam. 22.16. They largely illustrate how Yahwism's uncom-
promising monotheism absorbed but also changed that which was
incompatible.

Exodus 15.1-18,[3] 'The Song of Miriam', is a hymn of thanksgiv-
ing to Yahweh for his saving act at the Reed Sea. Verses 1-3 introduce Yahweh who has gained the victory over Egypt. Verses 4-12
have the recital of deeds customary in the main body of such a
hymnic psalm. Verses 13-17 continue this with a recital of post-
exodus events, concluding with the doxology in 18.

The verses under discussion here are 8 and 10:

8   At the blast of thy nostrils (ברוח אפיך) the waters piled up,
      the floods stood up in a heap;
      the deeps congealed in the heart of the sea.
9   The enemy said, 'I will pursue, I will overtake,
      I will divide the spoil, my desire shall have its fill of them.
      I will draw my sword, my hand shall destroy them'.
10 Thou didst blow with thy wind (נשפת ברוחך), the sea
      covered them; they sank as lead in the mighty waters.

---

[2] There existed in the world into which Israel was born two related concepts
which had bearing on Israel's concept of the spirit. The one has to do with wind,
intimately related to the world of the gods and serving as a messenger or divine
assistant, and in some instances at least, considered to be an independent deity.
The second closely related concept conceived of the wind as the breath of the
gods which had creative and life-sustaining power and which dwelt in each creature as the breath of life, giving life and strength as long as it was granted to the
creature. For Egyptian or Mesopotamian texts which illustrate these two concepts, see J. Hehn, 'Zum Problem des Geistes im alten Orient und im AT', *ZAW*
43 (1925), pp. 216-25.
[3] Cf. Frank M. Cross Jr. and David Noel Freedman, 'The Song of Miriam',
JNES 14 (1955), pp. 239-50, for a defense of the antiquity of this hymn.

The fact that the wind is mentioned in 14.21 leaves no doubt about its actual presence. But is it the wind that the hymn writer describes in 15.8-10? It is possible that the writer had in mind only the wind viewed figuratively as the breath of Yahweh. But there are indications that *ruach* in v. 8 and also in v. 10 means Yahweh's power.

The fact that *ruach* in v. 8 should be translated as 'breath' rather than 'wind' is determined by the word אפיך. This latter word could also have the meaning of 'anger'.[4] However, the 'fury' of Yahweh is directed against the Egyptians (v. 7) and not against the waters (v. 8). On the contrary, the waters almost seem to be a friendly participant in the struggle against the common Egyptian enemy, for the floods stand at attention (נצבו) as if they are members of Yahweh's army, and they are described by the quite complimentary אדירים (mighty) of v. 10. So the conflict is not waged between Yahweh and the sea but rather against the Egyptians. Therefore the אפיך should be translated 'nostrils' rather than 'anger', determining in turn that the *ruach* of v. 8 is 'breath', or 'blast' if one wishes to emphasize the power of the breath of Yahweh's nostrils.

The *ruach* in v. 10 is more difficult to translate. The translation 'wind' in the RSV is questionable for three reasons. The Old Testament in no other place speaks of Yahweh 'blowing' the wind. He 'brings', 'turns', 'makes' it blow, he 'hurls', 'appoints', 'raises', 'brings forth', but never does he 'blow' as if the blowing of the wind were equivalent to Yahweh's breathing. This would seem to indicate that *ruach* in v. 10 should be translated 'breath'. Secondly, because the writer meant 'breath' in v. 8, he probably meant 'breath' in v. 10, for it is the same action against the sea. Finally, the wind in the narrative account of Exodus 14 has no task that would correspond to the task of the *ruach* in 15.10. It is the *hand* of Moses that brings the waters *back,* 14.26-27. It is not certain that the wind was even involved here in the returning of the waters. For these three reasons it can be concluded that the writer meant the 'breath' of Yahweh in v. 10 also.[5]

4. So Martin Noth, *Exodus* (London: SCM Press, 1962), p. 124, 'the "blast of his nostrils" (v. 8) refers to his raging anger'.

5. For the translation of 'breath' in both vv. 8 and 10, cf. George Fohrer, *Überlieferung und Geschichte des Exodus* (Berlin: Alfred Töpelmann, 1964), pp. 113-14. v. 8 'Durch den Hauch deiner Nase', v. 10, 'Du bliesest mit deinem Hauch …'

By using *ruach,* the hymn writer meant to indicate that it was Yahweh's power, and not just the wind, that moved the water. Is it not conceivable that there is seen here the process, or the very end result of the process, by which the wind, viewed in other cultures as a divinity, is removed from participation in Yahweh's salvation acts, to be replaced in increasing measure by Yahweh himself, be it by his own hand, his own word, or his own breath? The divine wind in the Babylonian Marduk myth is of course subject to Marduk's control, just as the wind in Exodus 14 is subject to Yahweh's control. But in that polytheistic society it existed and functioned in the divine realm as a special instrument of the gods, a fact, moreover, which can be seen by its context in myth. An activity was attributed to the wind which was never to be found in the natural world, an activity which removed it from the natural world to the divine realm of the gods. Furthermore, in Egypt it functioned as a divinity in its own right as the god Amon. But Israel, at the same time that she made the wind nothing more than an element of nature in 14.21, has attributed to Yahweh himself, in 15.8, 10, the movement of the sea which resulted in the overthrow of the Egyptians. The 'breath' of Yahweh has assumed those functions assigned to the divine wind in other cultures. And the breath of v. 8 and v. 10 is no separate divinity, nor is it even separable from Yahweh. It is Yahweh's person acting alone to gain the victory as vv. 1, 3, 4, 6, 7, 12, and 18 emphasize. The glory is to be all Yahweh's. The victory is Yahweh's alone. There is no divine assistant.

This conclusion is underlined by the following observations. Psalm 18, dating from this same early period[6] and showing a situation in some ways similar to Exodus 15, has made the wind the vehicle upon which Yahweh rides (cf. 18.11, RSV 10). This indicates that the *ruach* of 18.16 (RSV 15) which acts upon the waters is not the wind at all but is Yahweh's breath, that is, Yahweh's power. Secondly, the Old Testament never describes the wind as the breath (*ruach*) of God. It does, on the other hand, equate the breath of God with the spirit of God[7] (cf. for example, Job 33.4 or 34.14).

---

[6] Cf. below, footnote 9, for the dating of this psalm.

[7] Isaiah 40.7 should be translated 'wind' rather than 'breath' for nothing more than the natural activity of the wind is present in the wilting of the flowers. Ezekiel 37 has the human 'breath' come from the four winds but does not speak of the breath of the Lord.

Lys has shown that the wind is never described in the Old Testament as a divine wind. It is only viewed as a created element in the natural world. In the later Old Testament literature it comes to be increasingly employed metaphorically to express vanity, emptiness, transitoriness.[8] So the demotion of the wind in Exodus 15 is not an isolated example but is the first instance in a process which continues throughout the whole Old Testament.

The use of *ruach* with 'nostrils' v. 8, and with 'blew' v. 10, could, at the same time as it recognized the fact that the natural wind blew (although this nuance is not to be taken for granted), also express the biblical writer's interpretation that it was Yahweh's controlling and active *power* which was present and evident in the Reed Sea event. Increasingly, in the course of the Old Testament literature, this unique power will come to be known as God's *ruach*, commonly translated as 'breath', 'blast', or 'spirit'. Here it was revealed in an unmistakable way to Israel for the first time in that once-and-for-all event which was so supremely decisive for the life of Israel as the chosen people of Yahweh.

2 Samuel 22.16[9] uses *ruach* in a context similar in certain respects to Exodus 15. The theme is the salvation of a king out of a dangerous situation. The actual circumstances are not identified but are rather described in semi-mythological terms as being a deliverance from 'great waters'. The verses under consideration are:

16 Then the channels of the sea were seen,
        the foundations of the world were laid bare,
    at the rebuke of the Lord,
        at the blast of the breath of his nostrils (מנשמת רוח אפו).
17 He reached from on high, he took me,
        he drew me out of many waters .

Determining the meaning of *ruach* is greatly facilitated by the presence of the word *neshamah*. This word is used in the Old Testament exclusively with the meaning of the physical act of respiration, so the phrase מנשמת רוח אפו cannot refer to wind and must be translated literally 'from the exhalation (or, power) of the breath

---

[8] Lys, *Ruach, le Souffle dans l'Ancien Testament*, pp. 337-41.
[9] For the dating of this psalm, a duplicate of Psalm 18, see, Artur Weiser, *Introduction to the Old Testament* (trans. Dorothea M. Barton; London: Darton, Longman & Todd, 1961), pp. 168-69.

of his nostrils.[10] This would serve as further substantiation for the interpretation given to Exod. 15.8 above, with which the present passage has in common the situation of salvation from the waters. But it differs in the fact that here, unlike Exodus 15, the anger of Yahweh, as well as his power, is expressed by *ruach* because *ruach* stands in a parallelism with 'rebuke'. This passage, in which the enemy is presented in terms of the mythological allusion to the sea, should offer the maximum possibility for the interpretation of *ruach* as the divine wind. However such a possibility is immediately excluded by the qualification of *ruach* with both אף and נשמה. Furthermore, the biblical writer, by giving the wind a decidedly minor role in v. 11 as the vehicle upon which Yahweh is mounted when he comes to save his king, means both to eliminate the wind from having any part in the combat against the sea and to reserve for Yahweh alone the role of victor and liberator.[11] So *ruach* here, as in Exodus 15, means the saving power of Yahweh, while in addition it bears the further nuance of anger or wrath. But any allusion to the wind is excluded.

B. Life-Giving Breath

The second main concept frequently found in ancient Near Eastern texts, the divine life-giving breath present as breath in the nostrils of every creature, finds no place in biblical texts of this period. Its nearest approximation is in Gen. 6.3, which together with the related text of 2.7, must be considered the transition texts of this period. But in the creation narrative in Gen. 2.7 (J), *ruach* is never mentioned, either as wind, as the breath of Yahweh, or as the breath in humans. It is as if the writer were conscious of and purposely avoiding the non-biblical idea of the breath of the gods present in every nostril, an idea which could have been readily suggested by the use of *ruach*. Nor does Gen. 6.3 serve as the point of introduction for entrance of this idea into Israel's literature. The unique spirit of God is not present in this text. Furthermore, the

---

[10] It is quite possible that the king, who has experienced a miraculous deliverance from the enemy through the intervention of Yahweh, has described his experiences in terms of Israel's miraculous crossing of the Reed Sea, cp. v. 16ab, only using terms which bear more direct reference to the Babylonian creation myth than are found in Exodus 15; e.g. 'great waters', 'rebuke'. The word 'drew me out', ימשני may also be a reference to Moses.

[11] Cf. Lys, *Ruach, le Souffle dans l'Ancien Testament*, p. 31.

very meaning of the text militates against the idea of any continuity between the divine spirit and the spirit in humans. The point of the text is that humanity cannot share in divinity in the manner suggested by the pre-biblical myth used by the biblical writer. The spirit in humanity is God's spirit in the sense that he is its creator and thus its possessor. The spirit in humans as well as their breath is derived from God, its source, through creation and not through emanation. The divine breath, the spirit of Yahweh, does not pervade the universe as wind in the natural world or as breath in the nostrils of every creature. It must be concluded that the emphasis in the Yahwistic religion on the unbridgeable distance between the creator and his creation precluded the development in Israel of any suggestion of the idea that the divine breath is present as wind in the natural world or as breath in the nostrils of every creature.

C. Origin of the Spirit of God Concept

There is to be found no concept in ancient Near Eastern literature which could have served as preparation for the spirit of God as it is described in the vast majority of biblical texts from this earliest period. The spirit of God as it appears on the elders or on the judges, on Balaam or on Saul, is a completely new thing without parallel or similarity in any extant ancient Near Eastern literature. If it can be concluded that Israel called Yahweh's unique power, evident at the Reed Sea, his *ruach,* his spirit, then Exod. 15.8, 10 together with 2 Sam. 22.16 can serve to describe the relation between the biblical spirit of God and related concepts in surrounding ancient Near Eastern countries. Moreover, they provide valuable clues pointing to the origin of the concept of the spirit of God. That is to say, even though the spirit of God came to Israel through revelation, yet Israel had been prepared for the understanding of this new thing by her acquaintance with the concept of the divine wind as it existed in the world into which Israel was born.

It has been argued that the spirit of God in the Old Testament was derived anthropomorphically; that is, as humans became aware of their own breath, they attributed breath to God in the same way that they attributed to God hands, face, etc. In time, as this breath in humanity came to be considered as spirit, so the breath of God in due time also became his spirit. The theory, however, that the concept the spirit of God arose as an anthropomorphism has been shown to be a highly unlikely one.[12] *Ruach* bearing the meaning of human breath is a relatively late idea in the Old Testament, and when it does appear it always signifies that which is weak and precarious.[13] For this reason it is not likely that it would have been attributed anthropomorphically to Yahweh. Lys prefers to speak rather of a 'theomorphism',[14] expressing the fact that the idea of the *ruach* in humanity was derived from the prior concept of the *ruach* in God and not vice versa.

Because of its obvious similarities to the pre-Israelite concept of the divine wind, Exod. 15.8, 10 points to the *divine wind* as the pre-Israelite background of the Old Testament concept of the spirit of God. But by the time of even the oldest Old Testament literature, the 'divine wind' and its functions has been absorbed into the Israelite breath of God concept. The source of the concept of the spirit of God is found in the pre-Israelite idea of the divine wind, but under the influence of the monotheism evident in the covenant faith, what was the source has been substantially and fundamentally altered to become that which the Old Testament describes as the spirit of God.

II. Innovation

New movements in their early untamed stages tend to be rough and violent with edges not yet rounded off. In contrast to the religious world in which it made its appearance, Yahwism was just such a revolutionary innovation. In keeping with its character as a new movement, early Yahwism frequently exhibited extremely vigorous and explosive characteristics. More often than not such violence and rude force is concentrated in contexts which relate the appearance of the spirit of God. The spirit of God displays the marks characteristic of this early period when it overwhelms and dominates its subject, when its appearance is rough and violent, or when the effects of its coming are only external or temporary.

---

[12] Cf. Lys, *Ruach, le Souffle dans l'Ancien Testament*, p. 335.
[13] Cf. Lys, *Ruach, le Souffle dans l'Ancien Testament*, pp. 348-59.
[14] Lys, *Ruach, le Souffle dans l'Ancien Testament*, p. 57 and *passim*.

A. The Spirit as a Dominating Power

Most of the texts of this period present the spirit of God as a power which in an extraordinary fashion possesses and dominates its subject, or which overwhelms the natural elements which stand in opposition. The freedom of movement is completely on the divine side and can in no way be controlled, coerced, or directed from the human side. The spirit moves where God wills and its coming can neither be anticipated nor precluded. The tendency of the spirit to overcome or master its subject is shown in the two texts from this period which describe the spirit in opposition to forces in the natural world, Exod. 15.8, 10, and 2 Sam. 22.16, discussed above. The *ruach* in these texts is as closely allied with Yahweh as his own breath. Yahweh's breath is the metaphor used to express the fact that the full force of Yahweh's power is exerted against the waters, in the one case for the salvation of his people and in the other for the deliverance of his king.

A majority of the texts of this period, however, speak of Yahweh's power, his spirit, in relation to humanity. The nature of the spirit as an overwhelming power is expressed in many passages in a great variety of ways.

One of the earliest texts in this period, Num. 24.2,[15] illustrates well this aspect of the spirit. Balaam, a Mesopotamian soothsayer, has been hired by Balak, the king of Moab, to curse Israel but is unable to speak anything but the blessings which Yahweh has put in his mouth (Num. 23.12, 26, etc.). In 24.2 there is a different rubric: 'And the Spirit of God (רוח אלהים) came upon him'. This might be interpreted to mean that because Balaam gives Yahweh's message and not Balak's, it is the message which has been inspired by the spirit of Yahweh. But because Yahweh is stated to be the source of the message in 23.5, 12, 16, 17, 26 without the mediation of the spirit, it is preferable to suppose that the spirit has brought on the ecstatic condition described in vv. 3, 4, which, incidentally, is the fullest description of an ecstatic condition found in the Old Testa-

---

[15] Cf. Weiser, *Introduction to the Old Testament*, pp. 104-105, for the early dating of this text. Cross and Freedman, 'The Song of Miriam', p. 240, see similarities between Exodus 15, Judges 5, and the Oracles of Balaam and consider them 'roughly contemporaneous, scarcely later than the twelfth century'. The prose introduction is to be dated later, of course, but would appear to be no later than the Samuel texts which also fall in this early period.

ment. This is substantiated by 24.1 which states that Balaam did not consult the omens as at other times but 'set his face toward the wilderness', perhaps indicating a position preparatory to the ecstatic condition. The conclusion that it is the ecstatic condition which is caused by the spirit of God is not contradicted by the fact that vv. 3-4 are repeated in the fourth oracle (vv. 15-16) but without the mention of the spirit of God. Verses 1-2 are probably meant to be introductory to both the third and fourth oracles, since there is no further introduction before the fourth oracle.

Thus in this chapter the spirit of God is thought of as having occasioned the condition of ecstatic sight under the influence of which Balaam sees visions of God and hears his word. In this sense, the spirit of God spoken of in v. 2 does not inspire the word as it did during the major prophetic period. It rather causes the 'enthusiasm' which typifies this early period.

In this text, which is the only non-eschatological context in the Old Testament that associates the spirit of God with a non-Israelite, the spirit of God takes possession of an unwilling subject and uses that subject contrary to his/her own intentions. This aptly illustrates the dominating nature of the spirit of God in this early period.

The same dominating characteristic is shown again by the suddenness and utter unpredictability of the spirit's coming. This element, which emphasizes the fact that the spirit cannot be conjured or coerced, is particularly evident in the text described above, Num. 24.2. It is also present in those texts which describe a concomitant ecstatic state called 'prophesying' (Num. 11.17, 25, 26; 1 Sam. 10.6, 10; 1 Sam. 19.20, 23). Finally, it is in those texts in the books of Judges and Samuel where, without apparent warning, the spirit comes on or possesses the human of Yahweh's choice: Judg. 3.10; 6.34; 11.29; 13.25; 14.6, 19; 15.14; 1 Sam. 11.6; 16.13.

Numbers 11.16-30 (E), which must be understood as the description of an actual event in Israel's history,[16] is representative of

---

[16] Numbers 11 is considered by some a late rewrite of the actual events described in Exodus 16 and 18. Because the Elohistic source is known to be interested in prophets and because neither prophets nor spirit are mentioned in the Exodus account, these elements of the narrative are credited with no historical basis but are considered to have been added later by the redactor. For example, Lys, *Ruach, le Souffle dans l'Ancien Testament*, p. 62, n. 1, calls it a new redaction of

those texts which show the unprogrammed (from a human stand-point) and so irresistible nature of the spirit. The narrative has to do with the choosing of seventy men from among those who are listed as the elders of Israel, the chosen ones to serve as Moses' assistants in leading the people. Yahweh himself promises to provide the authentication:

> 17 And I will come down and talk with you there; and I will take some of the spirit which is upon you and put it upon them; and they shall bear the burden of the people with you, that you may not bear it yourself alone.

Moses gathers 'seventy men of the elders', and they meet around the tent.

> 25 Then the Lord came down in the cloud and spoke to him, and took some of the spirit that was upon him and put it

---

Exodus 18 and appears to date it in the eighth century. Eichrodt, *Theology of the Old Testament* (London: SCM Press, 1961), I, p. 310, footnote, dates the spirit-possession much later. See also Lindblom, *Prophecy in Ancient Israel* (Philadelphia: Fortress Press, 1962) pp. 101-102, who considers it an aetiological narrative that 'cannot be utilized as a historical record and has nothing to teach us about the real origin of ecstatic prophecy'.

It should be made clear, first of all, that the only thing being defended here is the historicity of some event which took place at a time when the spirit was manifested to Israel with undeniably visible concomitant effects. Whether this event took place before or after Sinai is not relevant to this point and will not be argued pro or con.

If the spirit in Numbers 11 is to be considered a redactor's addition, four questions must be given consideration: (1) Although the E source is interested in 'prophets' (cf. e.g. Gen. 20.7, Exod. 33.11, Num. 12.6-8, and Deut. 34.10), in none of these passages is the spirit mentioned. Why should it be assumed that a late Elohistic redactor (8th century) has added the spirit in Numbers 11? (2) Why would a late editor living at a time when ecstatic prophets and 'prophesying' are in disrepute (see below Chapter 3) use this visible 'prophesying' as a sign of the charisma for the elders and for Moses (although Moses does not prophesy, yet it is the same spirit that is on him)? This process of discrediting ecstatic prophesying seems to be already under way by the time of Elijah and Elisha, who do not 'prophesy', perhaps due to the adverse influence of the Baal prophets (cf. 2 Kgs 9.11). At any rate, it is difficult to believe that, without a tradition like Numbers 11 already in existence, an editor after 850 BCE would want to provide this kind of authentication for Moses and the elders.

Is it possible to believe that a narrative such as Num. 11.26-30, including the names Eldad and Medad, was a later composition? Such an assumption raises more problems than it settles. It seems preferable to believe that at some point in the pre-Conquest history of Israel the spirit of God was manifested in Israel's midst in an undeniable and completely convincing manner.

(ויאצל מן־הרוה אשר עליו ויתן) upon the seventy elders; and when the spirit rested (נוח) upon them, they prophesied. But they did so no more (יתנבאו ולא יספו).

26 Now two men remained in the camp, one named Eldad, and the other named Medad, and the spirit rested upon them; they were among those registered, but they had not gone out to the tent, and so they prophesied in the camp. (27) And a young man ran and told Moses, 'Eldad and Medad are prophesying in the camp'. (28) And Joshua the son of Nun, the minister of Moses, one of his chosen men, said, 'My lord Moses, forbid them'. (29) But Moses said to him, 'Are you jealous for my sake? Would that all the Lord's people were prophets, that the Lord would put his spirit upon them!' (30) And Moses and the elders of Israel returned to the camp.

Several things are indicated here about the spirit. The verb אצל (take) used only four times in the Old Testament, can have the meaning of 'withdraw' but the meaning of 'withhold' seems preferable, on the basis of Gen. 27.36, 'Have you not reserved a blessing for me?' (cf., also Eccl. 12.10, 'I kept my heart from no pleasure', and even Ezek. 42.6, 'The upper chambers were set back from the ground more than the lower chambers'.) The verb in vv. 17 and 25 does not mean that Yahweh 'takes away' from Moses part of the *ruach* already belonging to him but that he withholds some of that which is constantly being granted to Moses to bestow it on the elders. The verb does not indicate that the *ruach* is a substance or free agent that Moses has at one time had in his possession, but that is now to be divided among the elders. On the contrary, the verb emphasizes: (1) that it is above all Yahweh's spirit to be bestowed by his own free decision on whom he will, be it on Moses or on the elders; (2) that it is not and has never been 'possessed' by anyone, even Moses, but rather that it is a constantly renewed gift which can be withheld in whole or in part according to Yahweh's decision; (3) and that it is the same spirit that rests on Moses and on the elders. The verb נוח 'rest' or 'remain', used in vv. 25 and 26 of the spirit, indicates the continuing presence of the spirit. Thus, the 'prophesying' which accompanied it ceased but the charisma of the spirit continued.

Just what form the 'prophesying' took is difficult to determine. Perhaps it was a type of speech or an ecstatic condition which was visible to others. That it was contagious but controlled is shown in vv. 26-30, for Eldad and Medad were of those enrolled. It is specifically related to the gift of the spirit in v. 25. It is in no way spoken of in a derogatory manner in this chapter, which leads to the conclusion that it was a concomitant and extraordinary phenomenon planned and given by God at this specific time to show Israel the reality of the spirit and the genuineness of the gift.[17] Without this visible phenomenon, the presence of the spirit would be difficult to verify, particularly when it is bestowed upon individuals for the first time in Israel's history. But the fact that the prophesying ceased would indicate that the prophesying was only given at particular times for verification of the authentic gift and in no way should it be considered the permanent accompaniment or verification of the spirit. The cessation of the external phenomena also shows that the vocation of the elders was not to be that of prophets but rather that the prophesying authenticated them as judges in the eyes of the people.

The explicit account in vv. 26-27 emphasizes particularly the divine initiative in the giving of the spirit, while the narrative as a whole shows the spirit to be a power which seizes and controls its recipient.

Because v. 29 alone in this chapter speaks of prophets rather than prophesying it appears to point more to the period of the classical prophets than to the period presently under consideration.[18]

---

[17] John Calvin, *Commentary on the Four Last Books of Moses* (Grand Rapids: Eerdmans, 1959), IV, p. 35, says, 'God kept the two men in the camp because he wanted to show all the people, who were not at the tabernacle, that he was commissioning the elders'.

[18] The word 'prophet' does not fit well in the context unless Moses means to say, 'Would that all the Lord's people prophesied …' in the same way that the seventy elders, Eldad, and Medad 'prophesied', as an external manifestation accompanying the gift of the spirit. There are no prophets elsewhere in this text, only elders who 'prophesy'. But this 'prophesying' is not the 'prophesying' of the classical prophets but is the translation of the word, יתנבאו which denotes a kind of violent conduct, perhaps 'raving', as the same word is translated in 1 Kgs 18.29. But if Moses did not mean 'prophesying' by his use of the word 'prophet', the only other explanation for the presence of the word is that it has been inserted later for the purpose of authenticating the ecstatic *nebiim*. Then there is left in this verse only Moses speaking well of the gift of the spirit and looking forward with anticipation to the day when all in Israel will receive it.

B. Violent Aspects of the Spirit's Appearance

Closely related to the tendency of the spirit to dominate its human subject is the rough and violent, almost brutal nature of the spirit in this period. This is indicated primarily by the words used to describe the spirit's coming, but its effects on the human subject are also often of a frenzied, explosive nature.

For example, Judg. 6.34 ('The Spirit of the Lord took possession of Gideon', וְרוּחַ יְהוָה לָבְשָׁה אֶת־גִּדְעוֹן)[19] uses the unusual verb לבשׁ which is the common word for 'to put on', 'to wear', 'to clothe', or 'to be clothed'.[20] The word was used to indicate not only the violence of the spirit possession, for the spirit seized Gideon to drive him on to his feats of military prowess, but also the fact that the individual was used as an instrument or tool by the spirit of Yahweh.[21]

In the case of Samson, Judg. 13.25, after reporting the story of his miraculous birth, states that 'the Spirit of the Lord began to stir him (וַתָּחֶל רוּחַ יְהוָה לְפַעֲמוֹ) in Mahaneh-dan, between Zorah and Eshtaol'. The verb פעם is used only four times elsewhere in the Old Testament, always with the meaning of 'to trouble' (Gen. 41.8; Ps. 77.5; Dan. 2.1, 3). Here it must mean a troubling of the spirit, an uneasiness which presaged the violent acts of physical courage which are to follow. The three passages, 14.6, 19, and 15.14, all use

---

[19] For the dating of Judg. 3.10; 6.34; 11.29; 13.25; 14.6, 19; and 15.14 cf. Weiser, *Introduction to the Old Testament,* pp. 149-53. Because the spirit of Yahweh is not found in the so-called 'Deuteronomic framework', but in the body of the narrative in every case, and more especially, because the spirit of Yahweh is not found in every narrative (not found with Ehud, Shamgar, or Deborah, which should not logically be the case if it were an editorial insertion), the conception of the spirit of God is assumed to be contemporary with the narratives themselves. They probably had their origin near in time to the actual events.

[20] The LXX translation, ἐνδυναμόω, is used in Lk. 24.49, 'and behold I send the promise of my Father upon you: but stay in the city, until you are clothed with power from on high'.

[21] BDB, p. 528, translates it, 'And the spirit of Yahweh clothed itself with Gideon' and says in explanation, referring to G.F. Moore (no documentation), 'took possession of him'. Martin Buber, *The Prophetic Faith* (New York: Harper and Row, 1949) p. 60, says: 'His stormy breath, "YHVH's *ruach,"* rushes upon His elect, seizes him, "puts him on" (Judg. 6, 34), and his sword is henceforth the sword of YHVH Himself'. Jacob M. Myers, *1 Chronicles* (AB; Garden City: Doubleday, 1965), p. 97, translates the same verb (in this case used of Amasai in 1 Chron. 12.19) in another way and says: '"A spirit clothed Amasai" is a most significant conception of inspiration and revelation in the Old Testament ... and may be a forcrunner of the idea of incarnation'.

the same formula, 'the Spirit of the Lord came mightily upon him (תצלח עליו)', the verb literally to 'rush upon', indicating again the violent manifestations of the spirit's presence. As with the verb 'clothe', it indicates that the spirit 'used' Samson in an external manner rather than transforming him by working within him. In each case Samson gives evidence of the presence of the spirit by, respectively, tearing a lion in two, smiting thirty men of Ashkelon, and breaking fresh thongs used to bind him.

1 Samuel 10.6 and 10 are part of the narrative describing the first anointing of Saul by Samuel.[22] The chapter begins with the anointing (v. 1). Then Samuel explains to Saul, in connection with the asses which the latter is seeking, that he will meet a band of prophets who will be prophesying, accompanied by music:

> Then the spirit of the Lord will come mightily (וצלחה) upon you, and you shall prophesy with them (והתנבית עמם) and be turned into another man (v. 6).

After further instructions in vv. 7-8, vv. 9 continues:

> When he turned his back to leave Samuel, God gave him another heart; and all these signs came to pass that day. (10) When they came to Gibeah, behold a band of prophets met him; and the spirit of God came mightily upon him, and he prophesied among them (ותצלח עליו רוח אלהים ויתנבא בתוכם).

It should be noted that the formula is the same here as it was for Samson in Judg. 14.6, 19 (and for David in 1 Sam. 16.13), indicating the same possession by the spirit and the unpredictability of its appearance. However, there is added in the case of Saul the 'prophesying' which was not present with the judges. Perhaps both the 'prophesying' and the exhibition of military prowess described in 11.6 were necessary to convince the nation not only that Saul was to be their leader after the manner of the judges, but that the monarchy was being inaugurated as a new institution in Israel.

1 Samuel 11.6 reads, 'And the spirit of God came mightily (צלחה) upon Saul when he heard these words, and his anger was greatly kindled'. He sets out to rally the men of Israel in order to

---

[22] For the dating of the 1 Samuel texts: 10.6, 10; 11.6; 16.13-14; 19.20, 23; see Weiser, *Introduction to the Old Testament,* pp. 162-67.

aid Jabesh-Gilead, besieged by the Ammonites. The similarity to the accounts of the judges is unmistakable and has been mentioned above. 'The suddenness of the onset of this divine power, the precipitancy with which it overmasters the human personality and the absolute control to which it subjects it' are particularly evident.[23]

Finally, there is the rather strange narrative in 1 Sam. 19.20-24. When Saul sends messengers to capture David, they meet a company of *nebiim* (prophets) with the result that the 'Spirit of God came upon the messengers of Saul, and they also prophesied'. This happened again to a second and a third group of messengers. Finally, Saul himself went to Ramah 'and the Spirit of God came upon him also, and as he went he prophesied, until he came to Naioth in Ramah. And he too stripped off his clothes, and he too prophesied before Samuel, and lay naked all that day and all that night'.

This passage represents an attitude, popular in Saul's day, in regard to the spirit, namely, that the coming of the spirit of God resulted in the ecstatic condition, or an abnormal condition called 'prophesying' (v. 20, יתנבאו). In its description of Saul's conduct it emphasizes the violent overtones in the spirit possession of this early period.

C. Externality of the Spirit's Working

Externality is a relative term. To speak of the externality of the spirit's working is only to compare it with later periods when the coming of the spirit worked profound and far-reaching changes in both humanity and nature. No such thing is evident in this period. This is not to say, however, that the working of the spirit was superficial. It was vigorous, powerful, and penetrating. The mighty waters could not stand against it. Balaam's elaborate preparations for conjuring up a curse against Israel were swept aside by the advent of Yahweh's spirit. The judges were possessed by the spirit and were moved to perform powerful military deeds. They became the inspired leaders of an aroused nation. So the coming of the spirit was not superficial nor was it ever characterized by weakness or timidity. Externality, however, expresses the fact that the coming of the spirit was almost without exception a temporary phenomenon; and

---

[23] Eichrodt, *Theology*, I, p. 315.

secondly, possession by the spirit worked no lasting or inward change in the human subject or in his/her environment.

In the Balaam narrative, Num. 24.2, the coming of the spirit is obviously only temporary. The unusual verbs used for the coming of the spirit on Gideon and Samson, 'moved', 'clothed', 'came mightily upon', indicate that this was not a permanent endowment, while the rather explosive effects of the spirit possession would seem to indicate the same for Saul as well as for the four judges. However, the definite statement in 1 Sam. 16.14. 'the Spirit of the Lord departed from Saul', would indicate that at least in his capacity as Israel's first king, Saul was thought to have received the spirit as a permanent endowment. Only if it were assumed that it was a permanent endowment would it be necessary to note that the spirit had departed from him.

The elders as well as Moses in Numbers 11 receive the spirit as a permanent gift, even though the prophesying is explicitly described as being only momentary. Finally, the charismatic spirit on Joseph, Gen. 41.38, and on David, 1 Sam. 16.13, are permanent endowments. The specific statement of 1 Sam. 16.13, 'the Spirit of the Lord came mightily upon David from that day forward', indicates both that previously the coming of the spirit (on the judges?) had been temporary but now on the contrary it was to be permanent.

In spite of exceptions, however, the large majority of spirit texts from this early period testify to the externality of the spirit's working by indicating that the spirit is a temporary rather than a permanent gift.

Another characteristic of this early period is the fact that the spirit works no essential inner transformation either in humanity or in nature. This is obviously true in the two texts which describe the spirit in conflict with the waters, Exod. 15.8, 10, and 2 Sam. 22.16. Many later texts relate the spirit to water, but it is almost always in a context of a great increase in fertility with a subsequent blossoming forth of the natural world. No such situation is described in this earliest period.

That the spirit works no inner transformation seems most obvious in the Samson narratives. It was not the coming of the spirit but rather the enslavement and humiliation at the hands of the Philistines which radically altered his character. The spirit uses him as well as the other judges in the manner of impersonal objects. No permanent change in Samson's character can be noticed as a result of the coming of the spirit.

The narrative in Numbers 11 does not make clear whether the spirit worked an inner change in the elders, nor do the texts which refer to David. And if Num. 31.16 can be taken as an indication, Balaam remained essentially unchanged, an outlander in the service of Baal Peor.

At first glance, it might be thought that the change of heart in Saul (1 Sam. 10.9, 'God gave him another heart') was due to the action of the spirit (10.10). However, the order of the verses shows that change came after Samuel's instruction, but *before* the spirit came on Saul.

The general impression left from the texts of this period is that the spirit possesses and uses its subject without effecting any basic transformation. In this sense one can correctly speak of the externality of the spirit's working.

III. Consolidation

From the days of the exodus down to the time when the Davidic dynasty was finally established in the person of Solomon, Israel went through a long period of adjustment and consolidation. For the first three centuries of her history, Israel tried a number of institutions in order to find the one that would make possible for her a viable existence in her own world. In the framework of the theocracy established at Sinai, Israel set out on her journey under the leadership of the covenant mediator, Moses. His leadership was soon challenged, however, by the pressure of an ever-mounting load of work (Exod. 18.13-26). By the direct command of Yahweh, Num. 11.16, the seventy elders were ordained to help bear the burden of leadership.

As Israel moved from the semi-nomadic life in the wilderness to a settled existence in Canaan, and with the death of Moses and Joshua, a further change in the leadership pattern became necessary. The book of Judges describes those charismatic leaders who were suddenly called forth from a quite ordinary environment to become the military and amphictyonic leaders in Israel. The institution of the judges lasted for more than 150 years, but with such a desultory type of leadership it became increasingly difficult for the young nation to maintain her religio-political independence. Judges 17-21 also indicates that there were periods of serious moral anarchy in Israel which called for a more persistent and centralized control. Under Samuel, religious conditions improved but the military situation remained ambiguous.

Answering to an increasing clamor from the side of the people, Samuel, again on the specific direction of Yahweh, sought out Saul and anointed him as the first king of Israel. Thus Israel again made a complete and very drastic change in her leadership system. But the charismatic nature of this institution was still temporarily preserved. In spite of the fact that an attempt was made to preserve the Saul dynasty in the person of Ishbosheth (2 Sam. 2.8-10), the Davidic charisma prevailed, and soon David was anointed king over all Israel. It was not until the anointing of Solomon that the institution of the dynastic monarchy was established in Israel, to persist in Judah at least until the exile.

In such a time of change and consolidation the need for divine authentication for each new institution or for each change in system is quite apparent. This divine certification was provided in a definite and sometimes very visible way by the gift of the spirit of God. In this early period the spirit of God is above all the charismatic spirit which stands in the service of the covenant. It is possible to trace the changes in Israel's institutions by the texts which speak of the spirit of God.

A. Divine Authentication

Although Num. 11.17 associates the spirit with Moses ('some of the spirit which is upon you'), the actual coming of the spirit on Moses is never described.

The same context describes the spirit granted to the newly appointed elders (vv. 24-26). It is given as authentication for those elders who are chosen to assist Moses, a divine authentication necessary at the inauguration of a new institution in Israel. But the spirit is not limited to this function. Verse 17 seems to imply that *because* the spirit is given to the elders, they will be enabled to assist Moses in 'bearing the burden of the people'. The gift of the spirit is the divine charisma, the added gift which is necessary to those who are to bear the responsibility of leadership.

During the period of the judges when Israel must again adjust to the introduction of a new institution, the charismatic spirit is again described as present on Othniel, Gideon, Jephthah, and Samson. The spirit of Yahweh grants the gift of military prowess to all four; but Judg. 3.10 ('the Spirit of the Lord came upon him and he judged Israel; he went out to war') indicates that not only courage and physical strength for war, but also the ability and wisdom necessary for judging the nation and for putting down idolatry were considered to be gifts of the spirit.

Strangely enough, the spirit is not associated with Samuel, even though he is prophet (1 Sam. 3.20, 9.9), priest (2.11, 2.18; 3.la), and judge (7.3-14). However, the authentication pattern is not broken by the absence of the spirit from the Samuel-related texts, for Samuel does not represent a new religious or political institution in spite of the eminence of his person.

It is necessary that Saul, the first of the monarchs, receive the confirmation of the charismatic spirit, and this he does, both in the manner of the judges (1 Sam. 11.6) and with the accompaniment of the 'prophesying' (10.10).

David, however, did not represent the introduction of a new institution, so it was not in this capacity that he was granted the spirit. Probably, each charismatically designated monarch in turn was intended to have the divine authorization implied by the gift of the spirit. Thus David received the spirit (1 Sam. 16.13), but Solomon, his *dynastic* successor, did not.

1 Samuel 16.13 uses the old terminology for the charismatic gift on David but with a new content and a new interpretation: 'Then Samuel took the horn of oil and anointed him in the midst of his brothers; and the spirit of the Lord came mightily upon David from that day forward' (ותצלח רוח־יהוה אל־דוד מהיום ההוא ומעלה).

Here for the first time the coming of the spirit is made the *result* of the anointing (without the 'prophesying') setting a pattern for the future. The visible phenomena such as 'prophesying', those special external concomitant effects worked by the spirit which testified to the presence of the charismata, will no longer be considered necessary for authentication of the leader. Instead, the divine election to leadership through the display of charismatic gifts is to be displaced by (or considered included in?) the divine election through the ritual of anointing. The free gift of the spirit has become institutionalized, programmed, and, as a result, it disappears for the time being from the monarchy, to reappear only in the Messianic age.[24] It is not in any way related to Solomon or to subsequent monarchs. This seems to be the point at which the spirit of God severs its connection with Israel's leaders, with whom it has been almost exclusively concerned in this present period, to appear in the following period on the prophets.

It can further be observed that the continuing presence of the spirit with David is explicitly affirmed. This would seem to imply that the word צלח has previously indicated only a temporary or transitory presence of the spirit in the case of Samson or Saul. Thus the connection with the charismatically chosen judges is maintained through the use of the same terminology, but the content is changed to mean a continuing and abiding possession. The fact that this is still the charismatic selection of a leader is further substantiated by the following verse (16.14), which states that 'the Spirit of the Lord departed from Saul, and an evil spirit from the Lord tormented him'. The spirit of Yahweh which bestows the gifts necessary for leadership cannot be given to two men, both supreme leaders, at the same time. Saul has been rejected by Yahweh, according to 15.26, and, although he continues to rule with the name of king, yet, another man has, in fact, become king of Israel.

The relation of this passage to 2 Sam. 23.2, below, must not be overlooked. Both have to do with David, one at the beginning and one at the end of his public life. 2 Samuel 23.2 underlines the statement of 1 Sam. 16.13 that the gift of the spirit on David was a continuing thing. It also shows that the charismata granted by the spirit extended beyond the divine designation of David as monarch to include also his gifts as a hymn writer.

B. Transition Texts
Two texts, 2 Sam. 23.2 and Gen. 41.38, while anchored in this early period, nevertheless point forward to the following period.

---

[24] Actually, this is the only Old Testament passage that makes the gift of the spirit a result of the sacral anointing ceremony (Isa. 61.1 must be considered metaphorical as well as eschatological). Anointing and the giving of the spirit are only loosely related in the Old Testament account to show that the coming of the spirit is free and cannot be controlled by or contained in a liturgical act which would insure the coming of the spirit. God retains the power of giving the spirit as an act of his free grace.

2 Samuel 23.2, 'The last words of David', introduces the spirit functioning in a quite different manner.[25] The relevant text is v. 2. 'The Spirit of the Lord speaks by me (רוח יהוה דבר־בי), his word is upon my tongue'.

The use of the preposition ב with דבר is unusual but not unique. The usual form is אל in the prophetic books, although ב is used frequently by Zechariah and is also found in Hab. 2.1 and Hos. 1.2. It is also used of the Lord's speaking with Moses, Num. 12.2, 6, 8, and by Micaiah, 1 Kgs 22.28. Driver, who has discussed this rather unusual form, concludes that the meaning is to 'speak with', as a superior to an inferior, although 'in or through' is possible.[26] The latter meaning seems to be supported by the accompanying phrase, 'his word is upon my tongue'. The unusualness of the ב with דבר and the fact that it is rarely used by the classical prophets, points to a form of inspiration which antedates the prophets.

It is difficult to decide, however, whether David attributes to the spirit of Yahweh prophetic inspiration or poetic inspiration. Normally, prophecy is a word of judgment or of encouragement received by the prophet for proclamation. This poem, however, does not contain the elements of a prophetic oracle. Although it is called an oracle in v. 1, as were many of the prophetic messages, yet in this case it is an 'oracle of David' and not an 'oracle of God'.[27] Nor does it have the nature of a prophetic 'message' to be proclaimed, but rather is a discourse on kingship, centering on the Davidic covenant (cf. vv. 4-5). This also would indicate that the spirit gives something other than prophetic inspiration. From the nature of the poem and because it is called an 'oracle of David', rather than an 'oracle of God', it seems best to designate this as poetic inspiration. David attributes to the spirit of Yahweh the gift of eloquence

---

[25] For the early dating of this poem, cf. Weiser, *Introduction to the Old Testament*, p. 169, and for a detailed defense of its antiquity, Otto Procksch, 'Die letzten Worte Davids', *Beiträge zur Wissenschaft vom Alten Testament* 13 (1913), pp. 112-25.

[26] S.H. Driver, *Notes on the Hebrew Text of Samuel* (Oxford: Clarendon, 1913), pp. 357-58.

[27] Procksch, 'Die letzten Worte Davids', p. 114, has shown the similarity between 'The oracle of David, the son of Jesse', and Num. 24.3, 'The oracle of Balaam the son of Beor', which latter he dates to Solomon's time. This unusual form, in which the statement of the oracle is part of the strophic structure of the poem, is not typical of the prophetic writings, where it rather stands as a superscription. It is found elsewhere only in Ps. 110.1 and Prov. 30.1. Procksch suggests that it is an old, pre-prophetic form.

which has made him 'the sweet psalmist of Israel'. But along with the gift of eloquence the spirit of Yahweh has also inspired in David the contents of his poem, which has as its central theme the everlasting covenant that God made with David. Does David mean to say that the covenant also was revealed to him through the spirit of God? Although not explicitly so stated, the poem as a whole might seem to indicate this.

To the degree that David was different from Balaam, the effects of the spirit on David can be expected to differ from its effects on Balaam. The effects are seen not in ecstatic conduct but in intellectual stimulation. Because this is still the early period, similarities to the spirit as it appeared in or on the prophets can not yet be expected. But neither are the 'enthusiastic' traits which are common to passages from this early period (that is, the texts from Numbers 11, Judges, and 1 Samuel) readily apparent in 2 Sam. 23.2. This text serves as the transition from the spirit as it is evidenced in this period to the spirit of the prophets. That is to say, actual 'enthusiasm' as related to the spirit is disappearing but prophetic inspiration is not yet present.

Another transition text, Gen. 41.38 (E),[28] can be understood as a tradition that reflects an Israelite rather than an Egyptian idea of the spirit. This verse is an exclamation of wonder and a proposal to choose Joseph as overseer, voiced by Pharaoh after Joseph has interpreted his dream and advised him to store up grain for the famine years: 'And Pharaoh said to his servants, "can we find such a man as this, in whom is the Spirit of God?"'

What is there in Joseph that is seen by others to be evidence of the presence of the spirit of God? Some commentators have interpreted this as the spirit of prophecy because of the well-known predilection of the Elohistic source for prophets and prophecy. But

---

[28] Without debating the date when the Elohistic source was put into writing, it seems possible to consider the Joseph cycle one of the traditions which was included in the E document, and as such, having a history of its own before the formation of the E document. Thus its date certainly falls within the limits of the present period. That this passage reflects an Israelite concept of God and the spirit is confirmed by W. McKane, *Prophets and Wise Men* (London: SCM Press, 1965), pp. 49-50, who sees in the presence of the spirit of God in this passage 'a reinterpretation of the vocabulary of old wisdom and an accommodation of it to Israelite piety'. For the relation of this text to Daniel, see below, Chapter 6, Section III.

there are indications that it is rather the charismatic spirit which has been brought into relation with the wisdom tradition. Joseph is presented here not as a prophet but as a wise man, who in his wisdom is superior to the wise men of Egypt (v. 8). G. von Rad has pointed out the similarities of the Joseph narratives to Egyptian wisdom and to certain elements in the book of Proverbs.[29] Joseph has received the training and exhibits the ability for rhetoric and counseling which represent the ideals of the wisdom school. Thus Joseph is here cast in the role of the ideal ruler (cf. 1 Kgs 3.8) as he might be described by the wisdom school. But something greater than wisdom is here. His talent at counseling the king of Egypt in terms that are coherent and convincing and his great gift of organization are understood as evidence that the spirit of God is in him. They transcend the gifts of an ordinary sage and are considered to be, instead, extraordinary gifts from God. The spirit in Gen. 41.38 is understood to be God's gift of special talent and ability. It is through the spirit of God that these gifts are made available to Joseph.

This can be said to be a transition text not so much by its similarity to the following period as by its dissimilarity to the other texts of this period. In this text, the only one that associates the spirit with one of the patriarchs, there is present the charismatic spirit typical of this early period. But there are none of the violent elements familiar to this period. Nor is the gift of the spirit temporary or fitful. It appears to be a permanent and penetrating endowment, in many respects similar to the spirit given to David as described in 2 Sam. 23.2 above. In this sense it points forward to the following period rather than testifying to the characteristic marks of the spirit in this earliest time.

---

[29] G. von Rad, *Gesammelte Studien* (München: C. Kaiser, 1958), p. 272.

3

'THE MAN OF THE SPIRIT IS MAD': FROM ELIJAH TO THE EXILE

I. Historical Background

With the abrupt entrance of Elijah into the royal court at Samaria (1 Kgs 17.1), a new and different phase of the spirit of God has been introduced. This period belongs above all to the great prophets in Samaria and Jerusalem who stood as Israel's conscience and witnessed to Yahweh's continuing love and impending judgment. And it is above all to the prophets that the spirit is related in this period.

In the three centuries between the emergence of the Omri dynasty and the fall of Jerusalem, biblical texts[1] which mention the spirit appear to be clustered about two of this period's three important historical peaks: the time of Elijah-Elisha during Ahab's reign (869-850 BCE); and the latter half of the eighth century with Amos and Hosea active in the north, Isaiah and Micah in the south (a period which included the dissolution and fall of the Northern Kingdom [722 BCE] and the Assyrian crisis in Judah under Ahaz and Hezekiah). The spirit is never mentioned during the third crisis period at the end of the seventh century, Jeremiah's time, which included Josiah's reform' (622 BCE), Jehoiakim's reign, and the first fall of Jerusalem (597 BCE).

Yahwism in the Northern Kingdom was threatened to the very core of its existence by Jezebel's attempt to introduce Baalism as the official state religion (1 Kgs 18.19) during the reign of Ahab. Her only effective opposition was the prophets and the prophetic

---

[1] The texts from this period: 1 Kgs 18.12; 22.24; 2 Kgs 2.16; Hos. 9.7; 13.15; Isa. 4.4; 11.2, 15; 30.1, 28; 31.3; Mic. 2.7; 3.8.

bands, although there were Yahwist sympathizers even in the royal court at Samaria (1 Kgs 18.1-4) and a hard core of the faithful who refused to convert to Baalism (19.18).

Without doubt, it was a time of crisis for the covenant people (19.14). This was not a crisis brought on by the threat of military conquest or by economic disaster. On the contrary, during the time of the Omri dynasty, Israel was able not only to defend her borders from foreign invasion but in addition, because of marriage alliances with Phoenicia and Judah, she was able to enlarge her borders in the direction of Moab and maintain a relatively high level of prosperity.

Israel suffered rather from an internal crisis of faith. So general was the apostasy that for the first time in the recorded covenant history the person of the prophet was described as endangered if he spoke out too vigorously.

To the prophets was left the task of defending the Yahwist faith based on the Sinaitic covenant. They came armed with the word and empowered by the spirit. It will be seen below what form the spirit of God took in this period. Texts relative to the period of the Omrides are 1 Kgs 18.12, 22.24, and 2 Kgs 2.16. It is significant that of the relatively few pre-exilic texts which mention the spirit, three of them should appear here clustered around events in the Omri period. The spirit is always closely related to the covenant events, and its appearance here can mean the reaffirmation of the Sinaitic covenant by the prophets and the reassertion of Yahweh as the sole Lord and sovereign of his people.

Not for a century is the spirit mentioned again in biblical texts. It reappears in the prophetic oracles of Hosea, Micah, and Isaiah, whose activity spanned the last half of the eighth century. This was again a period of great stress for the covenant people. Assyria had become a world power and a constant threat to the existence of the small states bordering the Mediterranean. For the first time in her history, Israel was faced with a problem of military defense that she was completely unable to handle alone by means of her own resources. On the one hand, she could choose to trust in the protection offered by Yahweh through his prophets. This protection, however, was conditional on her absolute obedience to Yahweh and his covenant, a condition she frequently seemed unable to fulfill. On the other hand, she could place her trust in military alliances with other west Mediterranean states, particularly Egypt. This latter course of action was constantly interpreted by the prophets as evidence of a lack of trust in Yahweh and was so denounced.

Failing these alternatives, and at times in spite of the alliances, Israel's fate could only be capitulation to or conquest by Assyria. In the case of the Northern Kingdom it was the latter which befell her in 722 BCE, leading to her subsequent extinction as a corporate people of God. For Judah this fate was only avoided by becoming an Assyrian vassal state during the reign of Ahaz (735-715 BCE), an act denounced by Isaiah as apostasy. Only the payment of a huge tribute by Hezekiah in 701 BCE spared her the treatment that Samaria had received.

It was against this background of military threat, and alliance with pagan neighbors, of apostasy and the memory of the covenant, that the prophets speak of the spirit of God. It is the spirit above all which represents Yahweh's protecting (or chastising) power, expressed most vividly by Isaiah: 'The Egyptians are men, and not God; and their horses are flesh, and not spirit' (31.3). Again it is the unusual fact that the only pre-exilic prophetic texts which speak of the spirit are concentrated in the oracles of Hosea, Micah, and Isaiah, all dated in this eventful half century.

The third main concentration of events in this pre-exilic period came toward the end of the seventh century with the emergence of Babylon as a world power (633 BCE), the Josianic reform (622 BCE), and the apostasy of Jehoiakim leading to the fall of Jerusalem and the exile (587 BCE). The spirit of God is never mentioned in the literature of this period.

II. The Great Silence

A. Mentioned Infrequently

One of the most striking characteristics of this period is the total absence of the spirit from certain bodies of literature and the relative infrequency of its appearance during the whole era. By actual count, it is mentioned only thirteen times in this period as compared with a total of twenty-five in the earliest period. This is the more remarkable when it is remembered that this is the great period of the classical prophets who are traditionally associated with the spirit of God.

As was mentioned above, it is only found in certain narrative traditions from the mid-ninth century and in the prophets Hosea, Micah, and Isaiah, all of whom are dated in the latter half of the eight century. This means that after 700 BCE until the first exile in 597 BCE (when Ezekiel uses it in exile) no prophet speaks of the spirit of God, neither Jeremiah, Zephaniah, Habakkuk, nor Nahum, nor is it in Deuteronomy (with the exception of the P source in Deut. 34.9).

Again, certain aspects of the spirit are avoided completely in this period. The prophets do not directly claim their own inspiration from the spirit. Micah 3.8, 'But as for me, I am filled with power, with the Spirit of the Lord', could be an exception but it seems more likely that the words, 'with the Spirit of the Lord', are a gloss.[2] 1 Kings 22.24, in a ninth century text, implies inspiration by the spirit of God, but Micaiah only lays claim to such inspiration in an oblique manner.

Almost totally absent from the spirit texts of this period is also the ecstatic condition or the bizarre conduct associated with the spirit in the earlier period (1 Sam. 10.10, 19.20). It is barely alluded to in Hosea 9.7 in a way that leads one to believe that contemporary popular opinion commonly made the association: prophets-spirit-bizarre behavior. But none of the pre-exilic prophets seem inclined willingly to claim for themselves spirit inspired ecstasy, nor, with the exception of Hos. 3.8, is such an association made in any texts of this period.

B. The Spirit and the Ecstatic prophets

There are several possible explanations for this unusual silence. In regard to individual traditions, perhaps Amos did not speak of the spirit because he considered himself by profession to belong to the peasant class and not the prophetic order (Amos 7.14). This is pure conjecture, however, as there is nothing to indicate that only those who belonged to the prophetic orders or who spent many years in the prophetic calling felt qualified to use the spirit of God concept.

The fact that the spirit of God is never related to a ruling monarch in this period is accounted for by the fact that with the beginning of the dynastic monarchies, the charisma-granting spirit is no

---

[2] Cf. Sigmund Mowinckel, 'The "Spirit" and the "Word" in the Pre-exilic Reforming Prophets', *JBL* 53 (1934), p. 205.

longer necessary for the legitimization of the king and so ceases to
be associated with the reigning monarch. That this was not necessarily the case in the Northern Kingdom, where the dynastic monarchy was an on-again, off-again thing, and where in many cases the
support of the prophets was considered necessary to secure the
throne, might indicate that the shift of the spirit away from the
monarchy in the direction of the prophets involved more than a
mere institutionalizing of what had previously been a matter of
charismatic selection. It is possible that it also indicates apostasy
from the covenant faith and a spiritual hardening in the monarchy
as a system, making it impervious to the working of the spirit of
God. At least one commentator has seen in Isa. 11.2 a reference to
this hardening in the historical kings which will be remedied only by
the coming of the Messiah.[3]

But this explains only in part the absence of the spirit of God
from this period. The main reason appears to be the general reaction against the excesses of the ecstatic prophets[4] with whom the
spirit continued to be largely associated in the popular mind. There
is some evidence that this adverse reaction had already started in the
time of Elijah and Elisha, of whom it is never mentioned that they
'prophesied' (יתנבא).[5] On the contrary, 2 Kgs 3.15 reports that when
Elisha heard the minstrel's music, 'the hand (יד) of the Lord came
upon him'. The use of 'hand' rather than 'spirit' represents a deliberate avoidance of association with the spirit which in similar circumstances brought upon Saul the ecstatic condition (1 Sam. 10.5-
6, 10). The fact that the 'prophesying', called 'raving' in 1 Kgs 18.29,
was practiced also by the Baal prophets would serve to bring it, and
the spirit commonly associated with it, into disrepute. There is at
least a hint of this in the story of Elijah on Horeb (19.9-12), for

---

[3] Volkmar Herntrich, *Der Prophet Jesaja* (ATD; Göttingen: Vandenhoeck &
Ruprecht, 1950), p. 210.

[4] Described at length by Mowinckel, 'The "Spirit" and the "Word" in the Pre-
exilic Reforming Prophets', pp. 199-227, but pointed out at least as early as 1904
by W.R. Schoemaker, 'The Use of רוח in the Old Testament and πνεῦμα in the
New Testament', *JBL* 23 (1904), p. 20.

[5] The *hithpael* form of the verb *nabi* usually, although not invariably, indicates
the ecstatic condition rather than the proclaiming of the prophetic word, cf.
BDB, p. 612. Cf. also Jepsen, *NABI* (München: C.A. Beck, 1934), pp. 7-8, who
has noted that in this early period the *hithpael* form only means 'to rave or to be
mad', and that it has consciously been distinguished from the *niphal* form which
usually means to proclaim the word of Yahweh.

even though it is obviously a 'wind' which is not to be mistaken for the presence of Yahweh, yet the play on the word *ruach* would not be lost on that generation for whom the *ruach* which caused the 'prophesying' would seem to be most obviously that in which Yahweh is not present. This becomes clear in 1 Kgs 22.24, where there is recorded the attempt to distinguish the *ruach* causing the 'raving' (22.10), and together with it the false prophesying (22.12), from the spirit of God which inspires the true prophets of Yahweh.

That this reaction against the *nebiim,* the ecstatic prophets, continued and intensified in the eighth and seventh centuries is indicated by certain texts in the prophetic books which refer derogatorily to these *ruach* (windy?) prophets, often with biting sarcasm. Micah 2.11 is just such a text: 'If a man should go about and utter wind (*ruach*) and lies, saying, "I will preach to you of wine and strong drink", he would be the preacher for this people!' Micah is saying, 'They use spirits (strong drink) to induce the spirit (*ruach*) but the only result is wind (*ruach*)'. Jeremiah has a similar reference to the *ruach* prophets in 5.13: 'The prophets will become wind (*ruach*); the word is not in them'. Those prophets who claim to be filled with the spirit (*ruach*) have instead become only wind (*ruach*), deluding both themselves and the people. Hosea 9.7b, 'The prophet is a fool, the man of the spirit is mad', if understood as Hosea's direct denunciation of the ecstatic prophets, would indicate the same biting criticism of these men. If, as seems more likely, the verse is the interjection at this point of the actual words of Hosea's heckling audience, then the words reflect the uncomplimentary association of spirit and prophet made by the ordinary Israelite. It cannot be supposed that in this unfriendly context, joined to the words 'fool' and 'mad', 'man of the spirit' was meant as a term of respect. It is also possible that the words 'fool' and 'mad' indicate a popular evaluation of any and all prophets (cf. 2 Kgs 9.11, Jer. 29.26). At the very least they include the ecstatic prophets whose unusual behavior would have been most likely to have given rise to this odious reputation.

If these texts indicate accurately the popular image of the *ruach* prophets: a fellow with rather wild and bizarre behavior, given to strong drink, laying claim to inspiration by the spirit, and constantly reciting (for a price) cheerful oracles, it is easy to understand the absence of the spirit of God from the oracles of the classical prophets of this period. The spirit had become a disreputable thing through popular association with the ecstatic prophets. Evidently the situation had become such by the time of Jeremiah that he felt it advisable to avoid mention of the spirit entirely as did also his contemporaries, Zephaniah, Nahum, and Habakkuk. It is even more understandable that no genuine prophet from this period would claim for himself inspiration by the spirit of Yahweh. Only if, like Ezekiel, a prophet could be transplanted into a new environment could he again feel at liberty to speak freely of the spirit of God.

III. The Spirit and the Great Prophets

A. Related to the Prophetic Movement
In spite of the fact that the spirit in certain contexts is studiously avoided by the prophets, yet its every mention in this period is invariably associated, directly or indirectly, with the prophetic movement. It is the spirit that controls the person of Elijah in 1 Kgs 18.12 and 2 Kgs 2.16. It is the spirit that inspires the prophets in 1 Kgs 22.24 and Mic. 3.8. It is a surrogate for the title, prophet, in Hos. 9.7. The remainder of the texts from this period, Isa. 4.4; 11.2, 15; 30.1, 28; 31.3; Hos. 13.15; Mic. 2.7, although not related directly to the person or work of the prophet, are related to the prophetic movement by their place in the prophetic oracles. It is the prophets, and seemingly the prophets alone, who speak of the spirit of God.

B. Designation of Charismatic Leadership
In the earliest period described in the preceding chapter the course of the charismatic leadership in Israel was traced by means of the gift of the spirit. It moved from Moses to the elders, the judges, and finally to the early monarchs. 1 Samuel 16.13, 14 also makes it clear that the spirit had passed from Saul to David. But from the time of Solomon the spirit is never again mentioned in relation to a reigning monarch nor is a king's successor ever designated by the gift of the spirit. As soon as the monarchy became a dynastic institution its successive rulers could no longer be charismatically designated. It had forfeited the gift of the spirit.

Shortly after the conclusion of Solomon's reign the Elijah-Elisha texts pick up again the theme of the charismatic spirit. That the texts from this present period are all related directly or indirectly to the prophetic movement perhaps indicates that the prophets are in this way designated the new charismatic persons in Israel, and if not the political, at least the spiritual leaders who are to communicate Yahweh's will and purpose to the covenant people. The spirit of Yahweh has moved from the monarchy to the prophetic movement.

Charismatic designation by the spirit was intimately related to the Sinaitic covenant. If the prophets were the successors of the old amphictyonic leaders, it was because of their emphasis on the sole lordship of Yahweh in an increasingly secular and syncretistic society. It was their call and task to be the protagonists and defenders of the covenant traditions. They were called to this task by the spirit of Yahweh and in the power of the spirit they superbly fulfilled their commission.

C. Inspiring, Empowering, Directing the Prophets

Yahweh not only designated by means of the spirit those who were to be his chosen instruments in the covenant community. He also actually worked in and through the prophets by means of the spirit.

1. Inspiring the Word

It is the unusual fact that there is only one pre-exilic text which speaks of prophetic inspiration through the spirit: 1 Kgs 22.24. This verse is part of the narrative account (vv. 5-28) that describes the scene when four hundred prophets assembled by Ahab unanimously prophesy a favorable outcome for Ahab's battle with Syria. Uneasy about this pleasant sounding oracle, Ahab, at the urging of Jehoshaphat, calls for Micaiah who is known for his oracles of woe. Micaiah, after predicting a disastrous end to the war, relates his vision of the divine council from which the lying spirit has been sent to put a false word into the mouths of the prophetic band. Zedekiah, one of the four hundred prophets, strikes Micaiah on the cheek as he challenges him with the words, 'How did the Spirit of the Lord go from me to speak to you?' (אי־זה עבר רוח־יהוה מאתי לדבר אותך). Micaiah replies that subsequent events will prove that the Lord has spoken through himself but not through Zedekiah. Micaiah is imprisoned but is vindicated by Ahab's death in battle at Ramoth-Gilead.

Even in this text Micaiah does not overtly claim to have received his prophetic oracle by means of Yahweh's spirit. But in a situation

where possession by the spirit carried with it a certain amount of
opprobrium, Micaiah's reticence in this direction is understandable.
Actually, under these circumstances, an implicit claim of this sort,
rather than an open assertion, has the flavor of real authenticity.

In at least three ways this text shows that it was a popular assumption that the prophetic word was inspired by the spirit of
God. The prophetic band, through their spokesman Zedekiah,
states as much in v. 24, '... go from me to speak to you'. Micaiah, in
his narration of the vision, recognizes that those present assume
that the spirit of Yahweh has spoken through the prophets and only
contradicts this belief to the extent of denying that this was the
true spirit of Yahweh. The belief that the word is inspired by a
spirit, even in the case of the 'weal' prophets, is left standing. Finally
the fact that he is challenged by Zedekiah shows that Micaiah is laying implicit claim to inspiration by the true spirit of God.

No other texts from this period show prophetic inspiration by
the spirit of Yahweh. It is possible that Num. 11.29, 'Would that all
the Lord's people were prophets, that the Lord would put his spirit
upon them!', is a text from this period (cf. Chapter 2, n. 18 and
text). But to date this text in the ninth century is to cut it off from
its context in 11.24-26 and to render unclear the function of the
spirit there. Whether it would still refer to the spirit which causes
the ecstatic condition, or to the spirit of prophetic inspiration, or to
divine power, cannot be determined.

Whether the claim to authentic prophetic inspiration as found in
1 Kgs 22.24 carried over into the eighth and seventh centuries cannot be clearly shown by any text.

2. Filling with Power

'But as for me, I am filled with power, with the Spirit of the Lord,
(מלאתי כח את רוח יהוה) and with justice and might, to declare to
Jacob his transgression and to Israel his sin' (Mic. 3.8). There is a
possibility that this text speaks of prophetic inspiration. It lies in a
context (vv. 5-7) which contains a condemnation of the false
prophets who prophesy pleasant things for a price but who denounce if they are not paid. The fact that this proves the completely
subjective nature of their oracles is underscored by the closing line
of v. 7, 'for there is no answer from God'.

Over against these weal prophets who cannot remotely claim to
have received their oracles from Yahweh, Micah sets forth his own
credentials in v. 8. However, just at the point where he could be expected to assert the authenticity of his own oracles he declares instead that he is filled with power necessary to denounce his people's
sins. This power is then further defined as the spirit of Yahweh.
Even though the context suggests inspiration of the prophetic oracle by the spirit of Yahweh, yet what is contained in this verse is actually an assertion on the part of the prophet that he has the power
to preach the truth regardless of the consequences.[6]

Even if the phrase, 'with the Spirit of the Lord', is an editorial
gloss, it would not alter the fact that here the spirit is used to indicate the moral courage that Yahweh grants to his servants the
prophets in the fulfillment of their commission. In this sense it resembles the spirit in those texts which speak of the empowering of
the judges and of Saul.

3. Under Yahweh's Absolute Control

1 Kings 18.12 presents the spirit in a strikingly new way. In the third
year of the drought which came on the Northern Kingdom because
of Elijah's word, king Ahab and Obadiah, his god-fearing chamber-
lain, set out on separate paths in search of water and grass for the
animals. Obadiah meets Elijah on the way and is requested to report
this fact to Ahab. Obadiah protests that it will mean his own life for
'as soon as I have gone from you, the spirit of the Lord will carry
you (ורוח יהוה ישאך) whither I know not; and so, when I come and
tell Ahab and he cannot find you, he will kill me, although I your
servant have revered the Lord from my youth'.

If Obadiah were talking about 'levitation' or mere transportation
from one place to another, 'wind' would be the likely translation of
ruach. A wind of hurricane proportions, or a whirlwind, would be
called for, but, neither of these is indicated in the text. There is also
no indication in the Old Testament that literal transportation of
men by the wind was ever considered to be a possibility. 2 Kings

---

[6] Micah 3.8 is the only place where the word power, or any equivalent word
having the connotation of God's power, is used together with *ruach*. This is surprising in view of the fact that one of the principal meanings of *ruach* is power.
Perhaps כח was associated in the popular mind primarily with human power. If
so, this might have caused the biblical writers to avoid placing it parallel with *ruach*
unless it could be contrasted with God's *ruach*. Cf. Zech. 4.6, Isa. 31.3.

2.11, the translation of Elijah, certainly does not indicate any such popular opinion nor does it actually have to do with 'levitation' or transportation in the ordinary sense of the word. Obadiah has in mind something other than mere transportation. This God-fearing palace servant is thinking of a recurrence of Elijah's mysterious *disappearance* (cf. 18.10), which could only be attributed to Yahweh's absolute control over Elijah's person (the *'ruach Yahweh* will carry you whither I know not'). He knows that Elijah lives in complete service to Israel's Lord (cf. v. 10), 'as the Lord *your* God lives'. So the emphasis is hardly on the physical movement of the prophet from place to place but rather on the fact that *Yahweh* can do with him as he wishes. Elijah, Obadiah says, is so completely at the disposal of God's will and power that nothing can guarantee his continuing to remain in this one place for any length of time. When so much more than mere physical transportation is meant here, including as it does the expression of Yahweh's personal and direct will and control in relation to Elijah, the translation must certainly be 'spirit of Yahweh' rather than 'wind'.[7] The word 'wind' could hardly serve to express the direct power and control which Yahweh exerts over Elijah.

This translation of 'spirit' is further substantiated by the fact that *ruach Yahweh* only twice in the Old Testament has reference to wind, Isa. 40.7; 59.19. Otherwise, without exception in its frequent appearances, it means the spirit of God (sometimes expressed metaphorically as the breath of God). Finally, the fact that 18.46 speaks of a similar action of God exerted on Elijah, this time using 'hand', shows that the power is more personally related to Yahweh than wind can be. It must be Yahweh's spirit.

This text emphasizes the powerful action of the spirit of God, controlling the activity of the prophet who stands in his service. Nevertheless, there is no indication that this control is more than an external control. The spirit handles Elijah like an object but nothing in the text indicates an influence on his inward being. Exodus 15.8 described the power of God directed against an inanimate object. Here the action is on humanity.

---

[7] Against N. Snaith, *The First and Second Books of Kings* in IB, II, pp. 150-51, and R.C. Dentan, *I and II Kings I and II Chronicles* (London: SCM Press, 1964), pp. 60-61. Cf., however, Lys, *Ruach, le Souffle dans l'Ancien Testament*, pp. 31-32, who understands *ruach* here as the spirit of God, also Jepsen, *NABI*, p. 22.

2 Kings 2.16 is similar to 1 Kgs 18.12. Elijah has been carried to
heaven by a whirlwind. The sons of the prophets ask Elisha's per-
mission to go in search of Elijah since 'it may be that the spirit of
the Lord has caught him up (נשאו רוח יהוה) and cast him (וישלכהו)
upon some mountain or into some valley'. As was the case with 1
Kgs 18.12, the reference is not to 'levitation' but rather to the absolute control exerted over Elijah by the will and the power of Yahweh. The translation 'spirit' rather than 'wind' seems even more certain here than in 18.12. In 2.1 and 2.11 it is the whirlwind, סערה,
that carries Elijah to heaven, a word frequently associated with
Yahweh and his theophany (cf. Ezek. 1.4) but unambiguous in its
meaning of wind, whirlwind, or tempest. If the reference in 2.16
were to the event of Elijah's translation and to the meaning of
'wind', the word סערה would have been used. But wishing to speak
of the spirit of Yahweh, they must use the ambiguous word *ruach*.
The meaning is 'spirit of Yahweh'.[8] The remarks made above in regard to 18.12 apply equally well here.

IV. The Spirit as a Medium of Yahweh's Work with Israel

It has been noted thus far that in this pre-exilic period the spirit is
only rarely mentioned, that the spirit texts are grouped at two very
precise points in the ninth and eighth centuries, that all of the texts
from this period are related to the prophetic movement to the almost total exclusion of other traditions, and finally, that a small
number of texts, mostly from the ninth century, relate directly to
the prophet himself. There remain, however, a number of texts
which bear not on the person of the prophet but rather on Yahweh's work with Israel.

A. Yahweh's Chastising Wrath and Saving Power
Why Isaiah should use the spirit concept when other pre-exilic
prophets almost completely avoid it is a question not easily an-

---

[8] 2 Kings 2 is full of interesting allusions. In addition to the whirlwind, סערה,
related to the Akkadian word for the divine wind, *saru,* mention is also made of
the *ruach* of Elijah in regard to which Elisha wishes to become his spiritual heir
(2.9 and 2.15). The manifestation of the spirit of Elijah (v. 8), which Elisha is
considered to have inherited when he parted the waters of the Jordan (v. 14),
seems to be an allusion to the dividing of the waters of the Reed Sea by the *ruach*
of Yahweh (Exod. 15.8, 10)

swered. He is the only one before the exile to speak of the spirit in the new age (Isa. 4.4, 11.2, 15). Perhaps Yahweh's spirit projected into the future would not bear the odious connotations that attached to the *ruach* prophets. It would seem more likely, however, that the spirit found its entry into Isaiah's oracles with his emphasis on Yahweh's sovereign power. With its background in the Reed Sea event and the empowering of the judges, *ruach* stood ready at hand as the prime term for expressing Yahweh's overwhelming power and irresistible sovereignty.

As no prophet before or after, Isaiah stood in the closest relationship with Judah's kings. He functioned as the king's advisor at a time when raw political decisions had to be made in regard to armaments, alliances, fortifications, all vis à vis the Assyrian threat. In opposing alliances with the western Mediterranean nations and dependence on any form of military might, Isaiah's constant theme in his advice to Hezekiah was the overwhelming superiority of Yahweh's power. This is given classical expression in 31.3: 'The Egyptians are men and not God; and their horses are flesh, and not spirit (*ruach*)'.[9] Judah, in the person of King Hezekiah in 705 BCE, is called to reject the proposed Egyptian alliance (30.1-5) and put her trust solely in Yahweh.

Isaiah 31.3 makes clear that the Egyptian military power on which Israel is depending is really weakness because it is not inspired by the spirit of Yahweh. There is no power other than Yahweh's spirit.

The antithesis is not between corporeality and spirituality but between power, which characterizes God and his *ruach,* and weakness, which is the fundamental characteristic of humans apart from the spirit of God.

Ruach here cannot be interpreted as either a substance or an entity standing apart from God. Both by the parallelism with 'God' in v. 3a and through the explanatory sentence in v. 3cd, 'when the Lord stretches out his hand, the helper will stumble and he who is helped will fall', it is indissolubly related to Yahweh himself. It can be said that there is no *ruach* but God's *ruach,* whether it be in humans, in creation, or in heaven. Thus the *ruach* in 31.3 is not a gen-

---

[9] For the authenticity of Isa. 4.4; 11.2, 15; 30.1, 28; 31.3, cf. Lys, *Ruach, le Souffle dans l'Ancien Testament,* p. 66, n. 1.

eral word for 'power'. It is power only because it partakes of and stems from the source of all power, God himself. *Ruach* apart from God becomes only wind.

Nevertheless, even though *ruach* can be said to be characteristic of God as *basar* is of humans, yet the prophet is not yet able to say, God *is* spirit. According to the terms of the equation in v. 3, just as Egyptians are not equivalent to horses, so also God is not equivalent to *ruach*. Absolute identity between God and spirit cannot be derived from this verse, nor can God be defined by *ruach*.

In another oracle, 30.28, Isaiah uses *ruach* to express the immeasurable and irresistible power of Yahweh, directed in this case against the nations. The same *ruach* upon which Israel can depend for her salvation can also be effective in the bridling and chastisement of Israel's enemies.

> 27 Behold, the name of the Lord comes from far,
>   burning with his anger, and in thick rising smoke;
>   his lips are full of indignation,
>   and his tongue is like a devouring fire;
> 28 His breath (רוחו) is like an overflowing stream
>   that reaches up to the neck;
>   to sift the nations with the sieve of destruction ....

Verses 27-28 stand isolated as a literary unit, having no discernible relation with what goes before or after. Leslie, joining verse 30 with 27-28, and relating the unit to 30.17, comments, 'the prophet uses the imagery of a thunderstorm as the vehicle of the Lord's judgment on Assyria'.[10] Fohrer relates vv. 27-28 more cogently to 8.7-8, where Assyria is pictured as destroying Ephraim under the same figure of the powerful, overflowing stream; or to 28.2, where both the thunderstorm and the raging torrent are used to describe Assyria.[11]

Yahweh's *ruach* cannot mean wind here, both because it stands as one of a series into which wind would not fit (name, nose, lips, tongue, breath) but also because it is likened not only to wind (v. 28c) but also to a stream (v. 28b).[12] The *ruach* is the power of Yah-

---

[10] Elmer Leslie, *Isaiah* (Nashville: Abingdon, 1963), p. 78.

[11] G. Fohrer, *Das Buch Jesaja* (Zürich: Zwingli Verlag, 1962), pp. 107-108.

[12] Hitherto, *ruach* has always stood in opposition to water, a position which hinted at the ancient opposition in the creation myths between the divine winds

weh,[13] here directed against the nations. It stands as close to him as his name, nostrils, lips, or tongue, all of which join in Yahweh's powerful and furious work. The reason for the destruction of the nations is not given.

B. Yahweh's Anger

Isaiah 31.3 and 30.28 use *ruach* to express Yahweh's great power, the former in the fact that he is God and not a human being, the latter under the figure of a surging, rampant river. There are other Isaianic oracles which express this illimitable power, but in which *ruach* is used to mean not power but anger, the angry mood in which he exercises his power.

In Isa. 11.15 the prophet has in mind Yahweh's action against the Reed Sea (Exod. 15.8-10),[14] although he preserves the imagery of 2 Sam. 22.16 (Yahweh's anger is directed against the *Egyptians* in Exod. 15.7, but against the waters in 2 Sam. 22.16). The verse describes a new Exodus when Yahweh will lead home the remnant of his people from Assyria, from Egypt, and from every nation (v. 12).

> 15 And the Lord will utterly destroy the tongue of the sea
>   of Egypt;
>   and will wave his hand over the River
>   with his scorching wind (בעים רוחו)
>   and smite it into seven channels
>   that men may cross dry-shod.
> 16 And there will be a highway from Assyria
>   for the remnant of his people,

---

and the primeval waters. Here, for the first time, water is used as a figure to describe *ruach,* thus suggesting a further demythologization in the abandonment of that rivalry, cf. Lys, *Ruach, le Souffle dans l'Ancien Testament,* pp. 83-84.

[13] Delitzsch, *Isaiah,* p. 40, says that these verses describe Yahweh as a man whose 'breath is a snorting that threatens destruction, which when it issues from Jehovah swells into a stream, which so far covers a man that only his neck appears as a visible half'.

[14] Note that in Exodus 15 both the hand and the *ruach* of Yahweh are present (cf. vv. 8, 10, 12); likewise in Isa. 31.3, where there is again a reference to Egypt, if not also to the actual Exodus event in 31.3b. Why should there not be found the same category, of *ruach* in Isa. 11.15 as there is in 31.3, the category of power translated by 'spirit'? Yet no one finds difficulty in translating *ruach* in 31.3 by 'spirit', even though the basic meaning is power. There should be even greater reason for interpreting *ruach* in Exod. 15.8, 10 as Yahweh's spirit after the pattern of Isa. 31.3, for in both cases the real opponent is Egypt which can be no match for Yahweh's power.

as there was for Israel when they came up from the
    land of Egypt.

The meaning of the word עים is uncertain, although the conjec-
tured meaning is 'hot'. The LXX prefers to read עצם.[15] As in 2 Sam.
22.16 the meaning of '*ruach*' is not 'wind' but 'spirit' (viewed metaphorically as breath). This is evidenced by the fact that it stands side
by side with 'hand', an anthropomorphism with which only 'breath'
or 'spirit' can suitably stand parallel.[16] In this verse where Yahweh
himself acts with no agent assisting (v. 15a), it seems preferable to
interpret רוחו בעים to mean a psychological emotion rather than an
instrument, meaning that he acted in hot anger for the sake of his
people.[17] The parallel passage, therefore, is 2 Sam. 22; 16, where the
ardor of his anger is expressed (perhaps similar to 'in the heat of
my spirit', Ezek. 3.14).[18] *Ruach* here is an emotion, a powerful emotion, an emotion which finds expression in Yahweh's action against
the water in the salvation of his people.

---

[15] For a discussion of this word, cf. Delitzsch, *Isaiah*, I, p. 292, and H. Hummel, 'Enclitic *mem* in Early Northwest Semitic, Especially Hebrew', *JBL* 76 (1957),
pp. 95-96.

[16] Cf. Lys, *Ruach, le Souffle dans l'Ancien Testament*, pp. 82-83. *Ruach* is an anthropomorphism in one sense of the word, but not really one, Lys explains, because one cannot describe God on the model of a man, for whom the breath is
essentially precarious and feeble. Lys prefers the term 'theomorphism'. It should
also be borne in mind that by the time of Isaiah the process of demotion of the
wind, begun already in the oldest texts, has progressed to the extent that Isaiah
only speaks of the wind, figuratively or literally, as a created natural element (pp.
77-79). To be sure, there is a mythological allusion lurking in the background, the
Sea and the seven-headed dragon, but this is even more reason to think that
Isaiah, in order to avoid possible confusion with the mythological wind, had in
mind 'spirit', 'breath', or 'anger' rather than 'wind'. The subtle play on words
would not be lost on his listeners, even as his not uncertain monotheism would
be fully evident.

[17] Cf. Fohrer, *Das Buch Jesaja*, p. 156, who translates, 'in der Machtfülle seines
Geistes'; and T.K. Cheyne, *The Prophecies of Isaiah* (London: C. Kegan Paul, 1880),
p. 77, who translates 'his violent blast'.

[18] This interpretation eliminates the difficulty posed by the concurrence of
hand and wind, if *ruach* were to be translated wind. Why should Yahweh need or
use wind as a duplicate weapon when his hand alone is sufficient elsewhere?
Translating רוחו בעים as an adverbial phrase describing how he waved his hand
eliminates this difficulty. The various readings suggested for בעים can all be used
in this interpretation with little change in meaning for the phrase. It is possible to
say, 'in the power of his anger', 'in the heat of his anger', or with Hummel ('Enclitic *mem* in Early Northwest Semitic, Especially Hebrew', pp. 95-96), 'his anger
boiling up'.

Hosea 13.15 speaks of the *ruach* of Yahweh as a destructive power, this time, however, directed against his own people:

15 Though he may flourish as the reed plant,
    the east wind, the wind of the Lord, shall come,
    (יבוא קדים רוח יהוה)
    rising from the wilderness;
and his fountain shall dry up,
    his spring shall be parched;
it shall strip his treasury
    of every precious thing.
16 Samaria shall bear her guilt ...

These two verses, 15-16, predict the invasion of the Assyrians under the figure of a scorching east wind rising out of the desert. Samaria will be denuded and will endure the most horrible cruelties (15d, 16b).

The RSV translation of *ruach Yahweh* as 'wind of Yahweh' is questionable. The subject of v. 15 is actually not a literal wind and a literal drought but rather the Assyrian onslaught and the subsequent spoliation of Samaria. This is seen, to be sure, under the figure of a scorching wind, but considered to be even more so the consequence of the wrath of Yahweh (cf. v. 14e and 16ab). So there is a strong possibility that *ruach Yahweh,* used in apposition to 'the east wind', was not meant to define the wind as such but rather was used to state the fact that Yahweh was using Assyria, the rod of his anger, as an expression of his righteous anger against disobedient Samaria.

This interpretation is supported by other considerations. Hosea only uses the wind elsewhere as a figure of futility (4.19, 8.7, 12.2). It is questionable whether he intends to give to the wind the importance it would assume if it were to be referred to as 'the wind of Yahweh'. Furthermore, not only in Hosea, but throughout the whole Old Testament, only twice is the wind referred to as 'the wind of Yahweh' (Isa. 40.7 and 59.19). In view of the tendency of the Old Testament writers to demote the wind, one can scarcely believe that Hosea, contrary to this trend, wishes to emphasize the position and importance of the wind by entitling it 'the wind of Yahweh'.

This indicates that *ruach Yahweh* means, not 'the wind of Yahweh', but rather 'the spirit of Yahweh', and can be taken to refer to his anger. Interpreted in this way, the passage resembles 2 Sam. 22.16, with the difference that there Yahweh's anger was directed against the waters *on behalf of* his chosen king. An even closer parallel is found in Isa. 27.8, 'Measure by measure, by exile thou didst contend with them; he removed them with his fierce blast in the day of the east wind'. Similarities in meaning are also found in 13.24 and 18.17. Jeremiah however never uses *ruach* to mean 'spirit', using rather the first person pronoun to indicate Yahweh's punishment on Judah.

Lys has pointed out the irony hidden in this verse.[19] Just as Amos had turned the Day of Yahweh, in which Israel had anticipated her own deliverance, into a day of judgment, so Hosea turns the *ruach Yahweh,* which in other days had signified Yahweh's deliverance of his people from the sea, into a destructive power directed against Israel herself.

Finally, in the same context of divine chastisement, Mic. 2.7 uses *ruach* to mean mood or temper but qualifies it with the adjective קצר (short). This gives it the nuance of 'short-tempered' or 'petulant'.

> 6 'Do not preach' – thus they preach –
>   'one should not preach of such things;
>   disgrace will not overtake us'.
> 7 Should this be said, O house of Jacob?
>   Is the Spirit of the Lord impatient? (הקצר רוח יהוה) ...
>   Are these his doing?
>   Do not my words do good
>   to him who walks uprightly?

Again, as in Hos. 9.7, there seems to be a literal record of the heckling carried on by the prophet's listeners, together with the prophet's rejoinder. Verse 6 records the people's protest against Micah's preaching of judgment, and their confident assertion that judgment will not come. To this Micah replies in v. 7 that what his hearers have just said should not be said. 'Is the Spirit of the Lord impatient?'[20] means, 'Is Yahweh bringing on this punishment due to

---

[19] Lys, *Ruach, le Souffle dans L'Ancien Testament*, p. 74.
[20] That this is the meaning of קצר רוח rather than 'restricted' or 'short in its reach' seems verified by the three other Biblical occurrences of the same Hebrew

peevishness or short temper?' The answer to be understood is, 'no', for the spirit of Yahweh is not like the human spirit.

Micah asserts that Yahweh does not act in this human way, striking out at someone in a fit of bad temper. On the contrary, he has been longsuffering and patient according to this promise in Exod. 34.6. The work of judgment is not his only work. He has also been good to the upright.

The spirit of Yahweh is to be understood here as meaning a psychological attribute. But in his manner of asking the question, Micah asserts not only that Yahweh's spirit is not impatient but also seems to deny the possibility of describing the spirit of God in terms of the human spirit or human conduct. The opposite must be true, that the spirit of God is the source, not the reflection, of the human spirit.

Ruach in Isa. 4.4 seems to refer more to Yahweh's anger than to his power. This passage ushers in a new role for the spirit, for 4.2, the verse beginning this literary unit, sets the *time* as 'in that day'. This indicates that these events are to take place in the future, in the new age.

Following hard on the denunciations and judgment declared in Isa. 3.13-4.1, the prophet abruptly introduces his listener to a future day (v. 2) in a purified Jerusalem 'when the Lord shall have washed away the filth of the daughters of Zion and cleansed the bloodstains of Jerusalem from its midst by a spirit of judgment and by a spirit of burning' (ברוח משפט וברוח בער). The verse undoubtedly is related to ch. 3, the filth (literally, human excrement) of the daughters of Zion referring to sins of the women of Jerusalem (3.16-24) and the bloodstains of Jerusalem to the iniquities of the elders and princes (3.14-15). The *ruach* of judgment and of burning must refer to the spirit of God, for wind cannot cleanse or wash,[21]

---

phrase, Exod. 6.9, Job 21.4, and above all, Prov. 14.29. Here it stands in contrast to 'slow to anger', ארך אפים. The RSV translation of Exod. 6.9 could well have been 'impatience' rather than 'broken spirit', for Israel, with her constant complaints against both Moses and Yahweh, seems anything but broken in spirit. For the translation of 'restricted', see Roland Wolfe, *Micah*, in the IB, Vol. VI, p. 913, and for 'short in its reach', see Norman Snaith, *Amos, Hosea, and Micah* (London: Epworth, 1956), p. 87.

[21] Cf. Delitzsch, *Isaiah*, p. 155; G.B. Gray, *The Book of Isaiah* (New York: Charles Scribner's Sons, 1912), p. 80; Volkmar Herntrich, *Der Prophet Jesaja*, p. 71; John

and the spirit in humans has neither the authority nor the power to carry out such a judgment. It is Yahweh who cleanses and it is inconceivable that his instrument, the *ruach,* would be any other than his own.

The 'branch' (צמח) in v. 2 identifies the future age of vv. 2-6 as the messianic age (cf. Jer. 23.5, 33.15, Zech. 3.8, 6.12, Ps. 132.17). In the messianic kingdom the messianic king will reign (v. 2a); nature will become wonderfully fertile (v. 2b); the remnant left in Jerusalem will have been purified and made holy (v. 3); and Yahweh himself will dwell in their midst (vv. 5-6). But the syntactical construction, אם at the beginning of v. 4, makes v. 4 the prelude to the situation described in vv. 2, 3, 5, 6. It is necessary for the Lord to purify the city of Jerusalem and its inhabitants as preparation for the advent of the messianic kingdom, in order that the remnant can be called holy and can endure the presence of the glory of God on Mt. Zion without perishing.

The spirit of God is to be the instrument which Yahweh uses for this purification. Yahweh must cleanse Jerusalem from the crimes of her leaders and the wantonness and pride of her inhabitants by his spirit which judges, condemns, and purges. The 'judgment' (משפט) refers to a legal decision[22] and indicates condemnation by the holy spirit of Yahweh. The 'burning' (בער) suggests purging and extermination (cf. Deut. 13.6 [RSV 13.5], 1 Kgs 22.47 [RSV 22.46], and Isa. 6.13). It is not an annihilation of Jerusalem's inhabitants, however, but a purging, preparing them for life in the messianic kingdom in the presence of Yahweh. As is true of the genitives in Isa. 11.2, the words 'judgment' and 'burning' do not denote qualities of the spirit but rather effects of its coming.

The spirit in this passage is closely identified with Yahweh, for it is Yahweh himself that cleanses. The spirit here indicates more than divine power, suggesting rather Yahweh's anger and passionate opposition to the evil which separates his people from his holy presence. This passage shows, for the first time, the spirit accomplishing an inward transformation in humans. It also shows the spirit to be holy, that is, characterized ethically. It also joins the spirit to the

---

Mauchline, *Isaiah 1-39* (London: SCM Press, 1962), p. 76, and many other for the meaning of 'spirit of God'. John Skinner, *Isaiah* (Cambridge: Cambridge University Press, 1922), p. 31, describes *ruach* aptly as 'divine energy'.

[22] Cf. G. Fohrer, *Das Buch Jesaja*, p. 74.

covenant, both the royal covenant (v. 2) and the Sinaitic covenant (v. 5) – 'cloud', 'smoke', 'flaming fire', 'glory'. But the whole passage, including the purifying work of the spirit, is only an anticipation of the future.

C. Yahweh's Mind

Yahweh's *ruach*, as used in the Old Testament, most often refers to his power, the divine energy, or to his wrath. But in Isa. 30.1 there is a most unusual meaning attached to *ruach*. It designates Yahweh's 'mind', expressed most commonly in Hebrew by לֵב (*leb*).

In this verse, Yahweh, through the prophet, denounces an alliance with Egypt, formed probably in opposition to Assyria's king Sennacherib in 705 BCE:

1 'woe to the rebellious children', says the Lord,
    'who carry out a plan, but not mine;
and who make a league, but not of my spirit (רוּחַ)
    that they may add sin to sin;
2 who set out to go down to Egypt,
    without asking for my counsel ...'

With the death of Sargon, king of Assyria, in 705 BCE, Judah became involved in diplomatic discussions with Egypt concerning a proposed alliance (v. 1, 'plan', 'league'), which would have as its purpose revolt against Assyrian domination. The political leaders of Judah, including Hezekiah, evidently knew already of Isaiah's opposition to their plan which called for a policy of political and military dependence on Egypt. Therefore, they have not consulted with him (v. 2) which, Isaiah says, is equivalent to acting without having received counsel from Yahweh. Yahweh wished to guide Israel in her foreign policy probably through counsel furnished by the prophet.[23] Israel's unwillingness to listen to, or even to consult, Yahweh's oracle is seen as rebellion against the guidance of Yahweh (cf. 'rebellious children').

The meaning of *ruach* in v. 1, however, cannot be decided alone from v. 2, as if v. 2 were merely a restatement of v. 1. At least three meanings of *ruach* in v. 1 are possible:

---

[23] Cf. Isaiah 37, 1 Kgs 22.5-28, 2 Kgs 3.11-27, or Jer. 38.14-28 for occasions when the ruling authorities sought counsel from Yahweh through a prophet.

(1) *Ruach* may refer to prophetic inspiration, readily suggested by
v. 2. In this case *ruach* would be the spirit that is the source of the
prophetic message, the inspirer of Isaiah's words of counsel which
Israel refuses to heed. This meaning is most readily suggested by
the conjunction of vv. 1 and 2, but it can be objected that nowhere
else does Isaiah speak of the spirit as being the source of inspiration for his own or other prophetic oracles.

(2) *Ruach* may mean the will or mind of Yahweh as in Isa. (see
below, Ch. 5).[24] This meaning would seem to be substantiated by the
parallelism, 'mine ... my spirit', in which the spirit of God appears
to be a part of the divine being. This would give the line the meaning that the alliance with Egypt is not according to Yahweh's *will*.
The principal objection to this interpretation, however, is that it is a
usage extremely rare in the Old Testament and, again, is never used
elsewhere by Isaiah of Jerusalem.

(3) *Ruach* may mean, finally, power. It was not by the power of
Yahweh that Judah had concluded the alliance with Egypt. True
enough, this interpretation is not readily suggested by the immediate context. But it is a noteworthy fact that in similar contexts elsewhere where Egypt is involved, it is the power of Yahweh that is
contrasted with the weakness of Egypt, most noticeably in 31.1-3.
It might seem, judging from the prophet's frequent use of this concept, that this is the meaning he has in mind for *ruach* here.

In spite of the weight of evidence for the third alternative, however, the meaning of *ruach* must be ultimately decided by the immediate context. If 1b and 1c are parallel, the meaning of *ruach* then
will be decided by the parallel member, מני. If the plan that Israel is
implementing is said to be 'not from me', it is not impossible that
this can mean that it is not *empowered* by Yahweh, but it is far more
obvious, and so preferable, to mean that the *plan itself* did not come
from Yahweh. Consequently, if the parallel line, v. 1c, is a rephrasing
of v. 1b, as it appears to be, then Isaiah is saying that the alliance
also did not come from Yahweh; it was not his will, but is quite contrary to what he had in mind for Israel.

---

[24] So interpreted by Jepsen, *NABI*, p. 16, n. 4, and by Fohrer, *Das Buch Jesaja*,
pp. 86-87 who translates it, 'die nicht in meinem Sinne sind', and comments, 'Da-
rum schmieden sie Pläne, die dem Willen des weltmächtigen Gottes nicht ent-
sprechen, weil er andere Absichten im Sinne hat'.

If this interpretation is correct, Isaiah is using *ruach* here to mean the center of volition in Yahweh himself, a meaning found elsewhere in the Old Testament only in Isa. 40.13.

D. Charismatic Leadership in the New Age

It was noted above that the gift of the spirit as the mark of charismatic leadership in the covenant community had suddenly been terminated with David. This indicated that the charismatic 'succession' from Moses through the elders and judges to Saul and David had ceased with the dynastic monarchy. The subsequent shift of the spirit to the prophets during the present period can be interpreted as meaning that the prophets had become Israel's charismatic leaders. After the prophets it is not easy to decide who, if anyone, actually received the baton of charismatic leadership.

Isaiah, however, in 11.2, takes up the theme of charismatic designation by the spirit and projects it into the new age. This text (Isa. 11.1-9) describes the coming of the future Davidic king, sprouting from a dynasty which has previously been cut off (v. 1, 'stump of Jesse'). His advent will mark the beginning of a reign characterized by justice and a righteous judgment (vv. 3b-5) and a paradisical realm whose features recall the original paradise existing before the Fall (vv. 6-9).[25] But at the center of the picture stands the ruler blessed by the spirit of God:

> And the Spirit of the Lord shall rest upon him,
> the spirit of wisdom and understanding,
> the spirit of counsel and might,
> the spirit of knowledge and the fear of the Lord (Isa. 11.2).

In this verse, Isaiah refers to charismatic persons in Israel's ancient past. Gifts bestowed in other days on chosen individuals for the temporary performance of a God-given task are now to be granted to the messianic king.[26] The spirit of wisdom (חכמה) and understanding (בינה) is a reference to the effects of the spirit of

---

[25] Herntrich, *Der Prophet Jesaja*, p. 209 sees a relation between Gen. 1.2 and Isa. 11.2 in that the restoration of paradise in 11.6-9 is a consequence of the presence of the spirit on the Messiah.

[26] J.A. Alexander, *Isaiah Translated and Explained* (New York: John Wiley, 1851), p. 163, says, 'The genitives do not denote qualities but effects of the Spirit ... This is evident from the last clause, where the fear of Jehovah cannot be an attribute of his Spirit, but must be a fruit of his influence'.

God in Joseph, the model ruler who was discreet (נבון) and wise
(חכם) – Gen. 41.39.[27] The spirit of counsel (עצה) could be a reference to the spirit which 'rested' on the elders enabling them to assist
(counsel?) Moses in judging the people (Num. 11.17). The spirit of
might (גבורה), which denotes physical power and courage, classes
the messianic ruler with the judges of the early amphictyony who
were moved to valiant deeds of courage by the gift of the spirit.[28] Is
the spirit of knowledge and the fear of the Lord a reference to the
special gift given David by the spirit of God (cf. 2 Sam. 23.3, 'ruling
in the fear of the Lord')? The charisma of the spirit had disappeared in the monarchy from the time of Solomon. This could
mean that the king no longer subjected himself to Yahweh, the supreme monarch. He ruled by right of birth and not through divine
designation. But now the gift of the spirit is to be renewed in fullest
measure on the new David. This renewal of charismatic leadership
means that Yahweh is in reality to be the leader and king, for he
now retains the authority to choose his earthly vice-regent through
the charismatic spirit.

Here, for the first time, the gift of piety, or faith, which is to
'know' the Lord and to fear him, is attributed to the spirit of God.
So an inner moral transformation takes place in addition to the be-
stowing of talents. Again, even though the spirit is a gift and cannot
be compelled, yet now the violent 'possession' of humans by the
spirit has disappeared. It is being replaced by the calmer 'rest upon'.
But finally, it is to be remembered that this activity of the spirit of
God was not realized in Isaiah's time but was only seen by him as a
vision of the future. The coming of the new age is to be characterized above all by the presence of the spirit of God with the messianic ruler.

---

[27] McKane, *Prophets and Wise Men*, p. 110, says that 'the ideal Davidic king is
portrayed in the vocabulary of wisdom as a sage. His wisdom is to derive from a
charismatic endowment (the *ruach* of Yahweh will rest upon him) and is associated with piety (even legal piety) … the fear of Yahweh …'

[28] Eichrodt, *Theology*, I, p. 309, suggests that the fact that the warrior traits
were included in the picture of the Savior Prince shows that these men, the early
judges, were considered instruments of Yahweh's dominion and genuine partici-
pants in the salvation history.

V. Conclusion

In spite of the apparent reticence of the prophets in regard to the spirit, the texts of this period mention the spirit in ways which show significant change from the earlier period.

First of all, the violent aspects of the spirit's appearance which were typical of the early period are no longer evident. Again, the spirit has shifted from Israel's amphictyonic leaders in the early period to be largely oriented in the prophetic movement in the present period. Related to the prophets it is described as inspiring their oracles and empowering them for the fulfillment of their commission.

In the early period the spirit was Yahweh's saving power acting on Israel's behalf. The same nuance carries over into the present period, but there is also a significant change in the fact that the spirit can become Yahweh's punishing and destroying power directed against his own people.

The charismatic nature of the spirit is maintained; but with the termination of the charismatic election of the monarchs it can only be viewed as a possibility for the messianic king, in a pattern, to be sure, which recalls Israel's earliest charismatic leaders.

Finally, the spirit has been redefined in this period in terms of Yahweh's mind and psychological mood.

Looking ahead, it can be seen that the writers of this period are working with a rather restricted concept of the spirit. The work of the spirit in the human subject is still largely external. There is still no evidence of the deep moral and spiritual changes to be worked in the one who receives the spirit (except in the messianic prince in the new age).

Neither is the spirit related in any way to the everyday life of the ordinary member of the congregation. The coming of the spirit is still a gift reserved only for that select person who is commissioned for a special task in Israel.

Finally, the spirit's relation to the created world is still only negative. The spirit opposes the natural elements which would hinder Yahweh's saving acts. No text has as yet described the spirit as an agent of creation.

4

'CAN THESE BONES LIVE?': EXILE AND EARLY RECONSTRUCTION

Israel in exile – that fact which should have been her *coup de grace* – acted instead to broaden and deepen her faith, the life blood of her existence. Jerusalem in 587 BCE was a city of death, Judah, a lifeless corpse. Small wonder that the people thus voiced their despair: 'Our bones are dried up, and our hope is lost; we are clean cut off' (Ezek. 37.11). But just as Israel, quickened by the spirit, was to rise from the death of the exile (Ezek. 37.14), so also Israel's thought life, the verbal and literary expression of her life before God, came to experience a renewal, a renaissance which resulted from the fatal catastrophe of 587 BCE.

That the exile stimulated use of the spirit concept seems proven by the fact that a majority of the texts from this period appear in books written by the exiles: 2 Isaiah, Ezekiel, and the Priestly source. In addition, Haggai and Zechariah, which together contain several spirit texts, were written by returned exiles. Perhaps the fall of Jerusalem and the exile, in their destruction of many of the old forms, permitted again the free expression of the activity of the spirit of God.

I. The Warp: Returns from the Exile

As the warp interlaces the woof on a weaver's loom, so the effects of this exilic renaissance can be seen moving through every category of the spirit's work. Certainly, new meanings are to be noted in this period: the spirit as an agent of creation and the spirit representing the presence of Yahweh. But even in these new categories, as well as in the pre-exilic descriptions of the spirit which have carried over into this period, the effects of the exile, the shock of this unparalleled disaster, can be seen. It is necessary now to describe those concepts particularly characteristic of the exilic period, concepts which exerted such a significant influence on the description of the spirit of God in this period.[1]

A. Emergence of the Individual

This emphasis can be noted already in Jeremiah's confessions (found interspersed among Jeremiah's oracles, chapters 11 to 20), a transcript of a highly personal dialogue carried on between Jeremiah and Yahweh. But the emergence of the ordinary individual from the corporate worshiping congregation could be expected with the fragmentation of the covenant community, the cessation of the centralized cult at Jerusalem, and the exiling of the mediating priesthood in 587 BCE. Again the problem of individual vs. corporate guilt must have been presented in acute form by the indiscriminate way in which the whiplash of destruction and exile fell on all, believer and non-believer alike.

This strain of individualism, absent in the pre-exilic spirit texts, is clearly evident in the spirit texts which date from this period. In Job 33.4, Elihu argues that he is flesh and blood like other men

---

[1] The texts from this period, dated roughly from 593-460 BCE, are as follows: Gen. 1.2; Exod. 28.3; 31.3; 35.31; Num. 27.18; Deut. 34.9; Isa. 27.8; 32.15; 34.16; 40.13; 42.1; 44.3; 48.16; 59.21; 61.1; 63.10, 11, 14; Ezek. 1.12, 20, 21; 2.2; 3.12, 14, 24; 8.3; 10.17; 11.1, 5, 24; 36.27; 37.1; 14; 39.29; 43.5; Joel 3.1, 2; Hag. 2.5; Zech. 4.6; 6.8; 7.12; Job 4.9; 26.13; 32.8; 33.4; 34.14; Pss. 33.6; 51.13; 104.30; 139.7; 143.10. The texts from the historical literature are all from the Priestly source, commonly dated to this period. For the early post-exilic dating of Isa. 27.8, cf. S.R. Driver, *An Introduction to the Literature of the Old Testament* (New York: Meridian Library 1956), p. 221. For the dating of Isa. 31.15, cf. Mowinckel, 'The "Spirit" and the "Word" in the Pre-exilic Reforming Prophets', p. 201, footnote 8. For Isa. 34.16, cf. Weiser, *Introduction to the Old Testament*, p. 193. The texts from Deutero-Isaiah are generally considered to be exilic, and 59.21, 61.1, and 63.10, 11, 14 can without hesitation be assigned to the exilic, early post-exilic period. Ezekiel's oracles bear dates ranging from 593 to 571 BCE. For Joel, cf. S.R. Driver, *Joel and Amos* (Cambridge: Cambridge University Press, 1915), p. 25. Haggai and Zechariah are both dated to the time of the rebuilding of the temple, 520-516 BCE. For Job, cf. Weiser, *Introduction to the Old Testament*, p. 291, or S. Terrien, *Job* (IB), p. 890. Individual psalms are almost impossible to date with any degree of certainty. Psalm 33.6 is dated to this period because of its affinities with Deutero-Isaiah and Genesis 1; Ps. 51.13 is generally dated to the time of the exile, cf. H.J. Kraus, *Psalmen* (Neukirchen: Neukirchener Verlag, 1960), p. 384. Psalm 104.30 has been included here because of its similarity to Genesis 1. Psalm 139.7 has been dated here due to its many affinities to the book of Job. Psalm 143.10 fits here as well as anywhere.

when he declares, 'The spirit of God has made me and the breath of the Almighty gives me life'. Another creation text in which the spirit is the giver of life, Isa. 44.3, says, 'I will pour my spirit upon your descendants, and my blessing on your offspring. They shall spring up like grass amid waters'. The personal nature of the spirit's work is most evident in the following verse, v. 4, 'This one will say, "I am the Lord's", another will call himself by the name of Jacob, and another will write on his hand, "The Lord's", and surname himself by the name of Israel'. Here is described the spirit's regenerating work in non-Israelites, joined as proselytes to the covenant community.

Individualism, particularly involving the ordinary member of the covenant community, is a cross grain moving through other categories of the spirit. The charismatic spirit, which had been reserved for Israel's leaders, is now claimed by Elihu in Job 32.8-10. 'But it is the spirit in a man, the breath of the Almighty, that makes him understand. It is not the old that are wise ... Therefore I say, "Listen to me ..." ' Elihu claims to have wisdom, not by reason of years, but because of a special gift of God through the spirit.

Joel 3.1-2 (RSV 2.28-29) promises the prophetic spirit to all classes in Israel. Sons and daughters, old men and younger, even slaves are to be visited by the spirit of prophecy. That God is present with the individual believer through his spirit is indicated by the psalmist in Ps. 139.7, 'Whither shall I go from thy spirit? Or whither shall I flee from thy presence?'

Finally, that God guides the individual believer through the spirit is indicated by Ps. 51.13 (RSV 51.11) and by Ezek. 36.27, 'I will put my spirit within you, and cause you to walk in my statutes ...'

B. The Inner Life

Texts which describe an inward moral or ethical change worked by the spirit in the human recipient appear in this period. In previous periods, Isa. 4.4 and 11.2 were the only texts which described this kind of a change worked by the spirit. The transformation described in texts of the present period, although given in terms of a more profound cleansing and renewal, is still only seen as a possibility for the future.

This growing emphasis on the inner life is one of the principal characteristics of the exilic period. Several factors served as possible causes of this development. The fall of Jerusalem and the destruction of Judah's national life must have led to much self-searching on the part not only of the faithful but of all who experienced this catastrophe. These repeated blows which fell on the body of the covenant people must have created the climate in which repeated prophetic exhortations towards inner cleansing could at last be heard not by a few but by many. The destruction of the external aspects of the cult as it was regularly performed in Jerusalem would serve to emphasize private worship and the development of the inner life of the worshiper.

In Isa. 32.15 the prophet describes the pouring out of the spirit as a result of which 'justice will dwell in the wilderness, and righteousness abide in the fruitful field'. The effect of righteousness will be quietness, peace, and trust. It would appear that the justice and righteousness would be effected, at least in part, by a change in the inner life of humanity accomplished by the spirit.

Isaiah 42.1 is a portrayal of the servant upon whom the spirit is bestowed. The fact that he will be patient, faithful, and persistent (vv. 3-4) can be interpreted to be the result of the work of the spirit within him.

Isaiah 44.3-5, mentioned above, describes the change wrought in the gentiles causing them to identify themselves with the covenant community.

Finally, in the most specific of these texts, Ezek. 36.26-32, after describing the new heart and the new spirit to be given to God's people, goes on to portray the spirit's work: 'And I will put my spirit within you, and cause you to walk in my statutes and be careful to observe my ordinances. I will deliver you from all your "uncleannesses".' Those who participate in the new covenant will experience this very inward, cleansing power of the spirit of God.

C. Turning Towards the Future

In times of stress there is always a turning towards the future on the part of those who wait for the Lord. This was particularly true in the half-century following the fall of Jerusalem. Every earthly reality that had provided support in the past, the king, the temple, the city Jerusalem, the cult, had been destroyed. No alternative to despair remained except the hope and expectation of Yahweh's renewing activity in the future. Thus it happened that some of the most profound expressions of faith found in this period are couched in the language of promise and projected into the future.

This is also true of the spirit texts from this period. Isaiah 32.15; 42.1; 44.3; Ezek. 36.27; 37.14; 39.29; and Joel 3.1-2 are easily recognized as containing this forward glance. God's people, together with the whole of creation, is to be renewed and transformed. Through the power of the spirit men will be able to walk in obedience. As a result of an outpouring of the spirit, all in Israel will become prophets and (as a result of their witness?) the nations will be brought into covenant with Yahweh.

But this glorious prospect in no way reflects the realities of the situation in which these oracles were spoken. The prophets who voiced these promises were looking into the future just because there was no hope in the present except in God himself.

D. The Universal Activity of the Spirit

Perhaps a mass exportation to a strange and foreign land was necessary for the breaking of the old forms. At any rate, this is the effect that the exile had on Israel. She was placed face to face with non-Israelite cosmogonies that were a direct challenge to Yahweh's sovereignty. This made absolutely necessary a statement or a restatement of Yahweh's universal dominion. The great emphasis on the creation tradition in Deutero-Isaiah as well as in the Priestly source and Job is the result.

This strain, which emphasizes the universal sovereignty of Yahweh, runs through the texts from this period. It is primarily the creation tradition texts in which this is seen: Gen. 1.2; Job 26.13; Ps. 33.6; 104.30; and Isa. 40.13. The cosmic aspect of the spirit's work is found in all of these. But Job 4.9, 'By the breath of God they perish, and by the blast of his anger they are consumed', in speaking about the retribution of the wicked, does not limit the spirit's work to Israel, and so indirectly expresses this universal element. Psalm 139.7 speaks of it most directly; 'Whither shall I go from thy Spirit? Or whither shall I flee from thy presence?'

There is another aspect to Yahweh's universal dominion which must have been a result of the exile. Living in a foreign land brought Israel face to face with peoples outside the covenant and forced a rethinking of Yahweh's relation to the nations. The answer for Deutero-Isaiah was the inclusion of the nations in Yahweh's salvation plan. This finds expression in Isa. 44.3, where, through the pouring out of the spirit, those peoples outside the covenant will be brought into it. In this way Yahweh's dominion will extend to the coastlands and to the ends of the earth.

II. The Woof: Life and Presence, New Patterns for the Spirit

Older categories used in describing the spirit at work, anger, prophetic inspiration, charisma, for example, naturally carry over into the exilic period. But two new and significant meanings appear in this period. One is the spirit as the giver of life, the agent of creation. The other is the spirit representing the presence of Yahweh with his people or with the believer.

A. Creator Spirit, the Giver of Life

Creation as a theme is present from the time of even the earliest strata of the Old Testament (cf. Gen. 14.22). But it did not become a major theme until the exile, a fact borne out by a comparison, for example, of Isaiah 1-39 with the exilic Isaiah 40-55. Just why the exile should emphasize the development of a cosmogony in Israel is of course only a matter of speculation. Perhaps it was caused by direct encounter with the New Year's festival in Babylon which celebrated the Mesopotamian creation myth, *Enuma Elish*. It is possible that Deutero-Isaiah or the priests felt it necessary to assert Yahweh's universal dominion over against the Babylonian deity, Marduk, by a more fully developed statement of Yahweh's creative work. It is also possible that the increased interest in history, especially in Israel's beginnings, that developed during the exile, as well as the interest in the end of history, would lead back to the earliest beginnings and would force the making of a positive theological statement in regard to those primeval beginnings.

Whatever the reason, creation emerges as a major emphasis in literature that has been dated to the exile – Job, Deutero-Isaiah, Gen. 1 (P), and some of the Psalms. In these writings the spirit of God is associated for the first time with the creation tradition, not only as the agent of cosmic creation, but also identified as the creator of humanity and the source of life in the regeneration of both humanity and the cosmos.

1. *Ruach,* the Agent of Cosmic Creation

(a) The central text relating the *ruach* to creation is, of course, Gen. 1.2. Because the determination of the meaning of *ruach* in other creation contexts depends to a large extent upon the establishment of its meaning in Gen. 1.2, this text will be considered first.

Arguments over the meaning of *ruach elohim* in Gen. 1.2[2] have centered on the problems: is *ruach* to be translated 'wind' or 'spirit'? is it to be taken with chaos in v. 2 or with God in v. 3? what function does it serve?[3]

> The earth was without form and void, and darkness was upon the face of the deep; and the Spirit of God was moving over the face of the waters.
>
> והארץ היתה תהו ובהו וחשך על־פני תהום
> ורוח אלהים מרחפת על־פני המים

In order to understand the context in which 1.2c is placed it is necessary to consider first 1.1 and 1.2ab, even though the interpretation of 1.1-2b does not seem to be decisive in determining the meaning of *ruach* in 1.2c. Genesis 1.1 has been interpreted either as a superscription to the whole creative process which follows in verses 3-31, or as a relative clause whose apodosis is either in v. 2 or v. 3.[4] That the creative activity of God is present in v. 1 and vv. 3-31 is never placed in doubt. For the interpretation of *ruach elohim* in 2c, it is not necessary to decide between the differing interpretations of 1.1.

---

[2] For a rather complete bibliography on Genesis 1, see Werner H. Schmidt, *Die Schöpfungsgeschichte der Priesterschrift* (Neukirchen: Neukirchener Verlag, 1964), pp. 192-200.

[3] Cf., e.g. J.M.P. Smith, 'The Syntax and Meaning of Genesis 1.1-3', *American Journal of Semitic Languages and Literatures* 44 (1927-8), pp. 111-14; *idem*, 'The Use of Divine Names as Superlatives', *American Journal of Semitic Languages and Literatures* 45 (1928-29), pp. 212-13; who suggested the translation, 'powerful wind'; Kurt Galling, 'Der Charakter der Chaosschilderung in Genesis 1, 2', *Zeitschrift für Theologie und Kirche* 2 (1920), pp. 145-55, who suggests that *ruach* is a part of chaos in v. 2 and that wind serves to fill the void over chaos; William McClellan, 'The Meaning of ruach 'elohim in Genesis 1, 2' *Biblica* 15 (1934), pp. 517-27, who decides on 'spirit' as God's creative power; and J.P. Peters, 'The Wind of God', *JBL* 30 (1911), pp. 44-54, and *JBL* 33 (1914), pp. 81-86, who wants to translate it, 'wind', as the vital spirit of the universe patterned after mythological thought.

[4] For a complete grammatical analysis see John Skinner, *A Critical and Exegetical Commentary on Genesis* (New York: Charles Scribner's Sons, 1917), pp. 12-14.

Genesis 1.2 has been interpreted to mean: (1) chaos,[5] either created, or, uncreated and so in existence even before the divine creative act; (2) nothingness,[6] the dark and neutral background against
which the creative act must be viewed; (3) the first step in the orderly creative process, assuming that 1.1 is an independent sentence,
and that v. 2 does not depict a chaos but the beginnings of an as yet
uncompleted creation.[7]

Ruach can only be interpreted as part of the chaos if it means
'wind', for the 'spirit' of God as it is presented in the Old Testament can manifestly be neither a created element nor an integral
part of primeval chaos. Syntactically, verse 2c belongs to the chaos,[8]
an argument in favor of translating it as 'wind'. Secondly, it has
been noted that the word מרחפת describing the action of the *ruach,*
is also used in Deut. 32.11 to describe the movement of an eagle
over her nest. This presupposes wings for the eagle and, by analogy,
for the *ruach,* nicely identifying the *ruach* in Gen. 1.2 with the wind
(*ruach*) to which is ascribed wings in Ps. 18.11 and 104.3.[9] Thirdly,
some have seen a point of contact with Phoenician mythology in
the mention of בהו as possibly related to Baau, the goddess of the
night and the wife of Kolpia, the wind.[10] This might suggest the
presence of wind in v. 2, hinting at the translation of 'wind' for
ruach. Fourthly, the fact that תהום is etymologically related to the
Akkadian Tiamat has been frequently noted,[11] leading many commentators to conclude that the *ruach* must be translated 'wind' as
the equivalent of the seven winds used by Marduk in his cosmogo-

---

[5] Thus, C.A. Simpson, *The Book of Genesis,* in IB, Vol. I, pp. 467-68.

[6] Thus Kurt Galling, 'Der Charakter der Chaosschilderung in Genesis 1, 2', p.
149; G. von Rad, *Genesis* (London: SCM Press, 1961), p. 49; Brevard S. Childs,
Myth and Reality in the Old Testament (London: SCM Press, 1960), pp. 42, 82, and R.
Kilian, 'Gen. 1, 2 und die Urgötter von Hermopolis', *Vetus Testamentum* 16 (1966),
p. 435.

[7] Thus Samuel Terrien, 'Old Testament Theology' (New York: Union Theological Seminary, unpublished classroom lectures), and Edward J. Young, 'The
Interpretation of Genesis 1.2', *Westminster Theological Journal* 23 (1960-61), p. 170.

[8] Cf. Brevard Childs, *Myth and Reality in the Old Testament,* pp. 32-33.

[9] Cf. Imschoot, 'L'Esprit de Jahvé, Source de Vie', *RB* 44 (1935), p. 490.

[10] Mentioned by Childs, *Myth and Reality in the Old Testament,* p. 32, n. 3, and
discussed by Skinner, *Genesis,* p. 50, and L. Waterman, 'Cosmogonic Affinities in
Genesis 1.2', *American Journal of Semitic Literature* 43 (1927), pp. 179, 183.

[11] Cf. W.F. Albright, 'Zabul Yam and Thapit Nahar in the Combat between
Baal and the Sea', *Journal of the Palestine Oriental Society* XVI (1936), p. 18, footnote.

nic struggle with the dragon Tiamat.[12] Finally, it has been argued that *ruach* is no more active than the other elements in v. 2, that God is described intimately and anthropomorphically throughout, so that there is no need of the spirit, and that the translation of spirit only came about in the later versions under Hellenistic influence. The conclusion for the proponents of this final argument is that only the wind is described here.[13]

On the other hand the arguments against the translation of 'wind' for *ruach* here appear overwhelming. First of all, in answer to the arguments of those who prefer the translation 'wind', it can be stated: (1) The *waw* in ורוח of 2c may be translated as *waw* adversative, 'but the spirit was hovering ...', separating 2c from the series in 2ab rather than joining it.[14] (2) However, even if syntactically v. 2c belongs to the statement of chaos in 2ab, this does not necessarily mean that the *ruach* is part of chaos as an equivalent element. It can just as well express an action of the *ruach,* conceived of as different in kind, over against the elements of chaos.[15] Moreover the fact that it is the only element in v. 2 which is described as active (with a verbal form not a copula) would favor viewing it not as a part of chaos but as quite distinct from it. (3) Although the identification with the wind through the verbal מרחפת is enticing, yet it is not decisive. The *ruach,* in contexts where it can be only translated as 'spirit', is often described by such anthropomorphic terms as 'leaped upon', 'clothed', and 'poured out', and the use of the verbal form implying the use of wings can be just as aptly applied to the spirit as to the wind. (4) Although a possible relation to Phoenician mythology has been noted, yet it is dismissed as unlikely, both because of the conjectural nature of the supposed affinities, and even more so because the available sources describing, the Phoenician mythology postdate

---

[12] Cf. H. May, 'The Creation of Light in Genesis 1.3-5', *JBL* 43 (1939), pp. 203-204; Harry Orlinsky, 'The Plain Meaning of Ruach in Gen. 1.2', *The Jewish Quarterly Review* 48 (1957-8), p. 177; E.A. Speiser, *Genesis* (AB; Garden City: Doubleday, 1964), p. 3; and Peters, 'The Wind of God', pp. 52-54.

[13] Cf. Orlinsky, 'The Plain Meaning of Ruach in Gen. 1.2', pp. 180-81.

[14] Cf. Umberto Cassuto, *A Commentary on the Book of Genesis* (Jerusalem: Magnes Press, 1961), p. 24.

[15] As Childs, *Myth and Reality in the Old Testament*, p. 35, has interpreted it, or Islwyn Blythin, 'A Note on Gen. 1.2', *Vetus Testamentum* 12 (1962), p. 121.

the Priestly source.[16] (5) Although affinities to the Babylonian creation myth are readily noted, most commentators are just as quick to point out decided dissimilarities. The Priestly writer has not taken over the Babylonian myth unchanged, but rather has used it as the foil against which its own creation account has been portrayed. This would lead one to expect not a slavish copying but rather a contrast.[17] Thus one cannot argue that because the wind is present as a major participant in the Marduk myth it must also be present in the word *ruach* in v. 2c.

Furthermore, other more weighty considerations against the translation of 'wind' must be taken into account. First, if *ruach* as wind is a part of chaos, why is it defined by *elohim?* It is impossible to translate *elohim* as 'God' in this case. An attempted solution was the proposal to consider *elohim* as an elative (giving it the adjectival meaning of 'mighty'), a grammatical usage not unknown in the Old Testament.[18] But two arguments weigh heavily against this suggestion. Although there are examples of elatives in the Old Testament, in no other place is *ruach elohim* used in this way, meaning a strong or powerful wind. Second, the Priestly writer would never have used *elohim* in v. 2 with a meaning different from that which he gives to it in vv. 1 and 3, without in some way indicating that it should be translated differently.[19]

If *elohim* does not mean 'strong' or 'powerful', then it must only refer to God. But 'wind of God' (or 'divine wind') cannot be an integral part of chaos and so must represent a power or force standing over chaos and acting on it. What then would its function be? It could scarcely be a drying wind for in the creative process the dry land does not appear until the third day. The wind could hardly be

---

[16] Cf. Childs, *Myth and Reality in the Old Testament*, p. 32, footnote; Skinner, *Genesis,* p. 50; Waterman, 'Cosmogonic Affinities in Genesis 1.2', p. 183. It may be possible to trace the derivation of these late Phoenician sources back to proto-Phoenician material but thus far, nothing to correspond to the divinities Baau or Kolpia has been found in the latter material.

[17] Cf. von Rad, *Genesis,* p. 88, Skinner, *Genesis,* p. 17.

[18] Suggested by J.M. Powis Smith, 'The Syntax and Meaning of Genesis 1.1-3', pp. 111-14, and seriously questioned by D. Winton Thomas, 'A Consideration of some Unusual ways of Expressing the Superlative in Hebrew', *Vetus Testamentum* 3 (1953), pp. 215-19.

[19] Pointed out by Sabatino Moscati, 'The Wind in Biblical and Phoenician Cosmogony', *JBL* 56 (1947), pp. 306-307, and in a different context, by Childs, *Myth and Reality in the Old Testament*, p. 35.

given a creative function, for the wind in the Old Testament is never allowed to participate in the creative process. On the contrary, by the time of the exile, the wind has been demoted and naturalized, perhaps as a reaction against just such a divine wind concept as is described in the Marduk myth. It is possible to believe that the *ruach elohim* is the Priestly writer's counterpart to the divine wind in the Marduk myth, but it is difficult to believe that the writer was using it to mean 'wind of God', a phrase which would be unique in the whole Old Testament. This argument alone, viz., the use of the wind in the Old Testament, seems decisive against the translation of 'wind' in v. 2c.

What then can be said in favor of the translation 'spirit'? Perhaps the strongest argument exists in those creation texts which date from approximately the same period as the Priestly source: Isa. 40.13, Ps. 33.6, Job 26.13.[20] All of them use *ruach* not as a created element, but as a creating power. *Ruach* in the first two, without question, cannot be translated as 'wind' while the third, though somewhat ambiguous, should be translated 'breath' or 'spirit' rather than wind. These three texts, all of which show definite affinities to Genesis 1 and have either influenced or been influenced by that account, [21] should be given due weight in the interpretation of Gen. 1.2.

Directly related to the reference in Ps. 33.6 is the function of the *ruach.* It has been objected[22] that the *ruach,* as spirit, in Gen. 1.2 serves no purpose, performs no useful function the results of which can be noted in the following verses. It is precisely at this point, though, that the translation of 'spirit' for *ruach* seems to be far superior to 'wind'. There is no good explanation for the appearance of *wind* among the formless elements of the primeval cosmos described in v. 2, nor does it ever reappear in the remainder of the creation account in Genesis 1. But the spirit of God, not at all out of harmony with the spirit of God that has been described from

---

[20] Cf. also Ps. 104.7, which does not have *ruach* but does have גערתך (compare with Ps. 18.16) expressing both Yahweh's anger (*ruach*) and his breath (*ruach*) used in uttering the word (cf. Ps. 33.6) which rolls back the primeval waters.

[21] Childs, *Myth and Reality in the Old Testament,* p. 32, says, 'the Priestly writer already had the example of Second Isaiah to follow', and W. Eichrodt, *Theology,* II, p. 49, says that Psalm 33 is in clear dependence on the Priestly creation account.

[22] Particularly by Orlinsky, *Myth and Reality in the Old Testament,* p. 180, but also by Skinner, *Genesis,* p. 18, and von Rad, *Genesis,* p. 48.

the earliest writings of the Old Testament, not only joins the God of creation in v. 1 to the same God in v. 3, maintaining the continued action of the creative God of v. 1 over against the chaos,[23] but also in harmony with Ps. 33.6, finds its direct issuance in the creative word of v. 3. On the one hand, the spirit of God is the creative power of God which joins with the word, bearing and articulating it, in the creative act.[24] On the other hand, the word communicates and authenticates the spirit, making it specific and concrete ('Let there be light'), a fact which served the pre-exilic prophets well in distinguishing the spirit. Particularly in this passage, the word safeguards the spirit from interpretation as an emanation,[25] the divine fiat revealing that the true nature of spirit is power at work in creation.

Finally, the translation of 'spirit' for *ruach* best explains the meaning of the word מרחפת.[26] The verb is found only once again in the Old Testament, Deut. 32.11, in the context of the description of a mother eagle teaching her young to fly.[27] This meaning is confirmed by the Ras Shamra texts,[28] where *rahaph* is used to describe the hovering or soaring of eagles and hawks (and the goddess Anat). Its occurrence in Deut. 32.11 suggests the loving concern of a mother for her young, the hovering movement of the mother bird over the nest of her fledgling young. The word seems singularly unsuitable for expressing the furious combat of the wind against Tiamat as it is described in the Babylonian myth. Thus it cannot be used as an argument for the translation of 'wind' for *ruach*, a ('translation used by those who would see in 1.2 a reference to this

---

[23] Thus Childs, *Myth and Reality in the Old Testament*, p. 35, and Kilian, 'Gen. 1, 2 und die Urgötter von Hermopolis', p. 435, who believes that 1.2 was interpolated for this purpose.

[24] The relation between the spirit and the word in this passage has been noted by Robert Koch, *Geist und Messias* (Wien: Verlag Herder, 1950), p. 22, by Hehn, 'Zum Problem des Geistes im alten Orient und im AT', p. 220, and by Terrien, 'Old Testament Theology'. For an essay on the relation between the *ruach* and the Word, with particular reference to Gen. 1.2, see André Néher, *L'Essence du Prophétisme* (Paris: Presses Universitaires de France, 1955), pp. 105-15.

[25] Thus Terrien, 'Old Testament Theology'.

[26] For a discussion of the word, cf. Childs, *Myth and Reality in the Old Testament*, p. 33, n. 2.

[27] Cf. BDB, p. 934.

[28] Cf. Driver, *Canaanite Myths and Legends* (Edinburgh: T&T Clark, 1956), pp. 56-59, Aqhat III i 20, 21, 31, 32.

myth).[29] On the contrary, this verb fits better the translation of 'spirit' for *ruach*. Lys has noted the salvation context of Deut. 32.11, as well as of the related passage, Exod. 19.4 (' I bore you on eagles' wings').[30] This expresses well the function of the spirit of God in Gen. 1.2. The creation by God is a transformation of the cosmos from darkness, formlessness, and chaos. Just as Yahweh, likened to a mother eagle in Deut. 32.10-11, cares for the infant Israel, 'the work of his hands', saving her from 'the howling waste' of the wilderness, so Yahweh, directly through his own spirit, transforms the as yet unformed cosmos from chaos, darkness, and formlessness. In both passages the word expresses the loving concern of the creator brought to bear upon the yet undeveloped creature. In Gen. 1.2c this loving concern is joined with the spirit, his directing, guiding, and life-giving power, to act upon the formless mass of 1.2ab.

In summary, arguments against the translation of 'wind' for *ruach elohim* in Gen. 1.2 leave as the only possibility the translation, 'spirit of God'. Because it is the spirit of God, it shows it to be related to the God of creation of vv. 1 and 3. The relation of the spirit to the word, noted elsewhere in the Old Testament, prevents the isolation of 1.2 as a separate or unrelated activity; it instead gives the creative work of the spirit its continuance and fulfillment in the divine word of v. 3. The verbal מרחפת, according to the analogy of Deut. 32.11, places the creative activity of the spirit of God in a salvation context. The *ruach elohim* is the life-giving power of God through which God works to bring into being his creation.

(b) Psalm 33.6, a hymn, makes explicit what was seen to be implicit in Gen 1.2. 'By the word of the Lord the heavens were made, and all their host by the breath of his mouth' (ברוח פיו). The spirit of Yahweh participates in the creation. It is his power whereby he created the heaven and its hosts. It is the breath which pronounces and bears the word of command. But this is a poetic way of stating that the life-giving spirit was the means by which God created the heavens and the earth.

There is a reference here to Gen. 2.7, where God is said to have breathed life into his creation. But the presence of the word establishes and protects the sovereignty of Yahweh. Spirit and nature

---

[29] Against Waterman, 'Cosmogonic Affinities in Genesis 1.2', p. 183, who would translate it, 'rush upon', 'dash at'.

[30] Waterman, 'Cosmogonic Affinities in Genesis 1.2', pp. 178-83.

cannot be identified, nor can nature be said to share in the divinity of the Lord.[31]

(c) Job 26.13 has reference to the activity of God's spirit in creation, but expresses it with mythological terminology:

> 12 By his power he stilled the sea,
>   by his understanding he smote Rahab.
> 13 By his wind the heavens were made fair;
>   (ברוחו שמים שפדה)
>   his hand pierced the fleeing serpent.

There is an allusion here both to the natural wind which clears the skies after a storm, as well as the divine wind which drove away the dragon overshadowing the sun.[32] The mythology, however, is only the vehicle by which the poet describes the creation of light and an orderly universe[33] through the power of God's spirit (v. 13a). That this is true seems sufficiently indicated by the series: 'power', 'understanding', '*ruach*', 'hand', where *ruach* translated as 'wind' would be out of place. The writer has intended to convey the thought that something as personally related to the deity as 'power', 'understanding', 'hand', was meant by *ruach*. So *ruach* should be translated 'breath', and can only mean the spirit of God, the creative and life-giving power of God (cf. v. 14c). The biblical writer, furthermore, has been anxious to avoid associating the wind and the dragon, the classic enemies of the pagan mythologies. The other three terms, 'power', 'understanding', and 'hand' (that is, God himself) stand in opposition to the sea-Rahab-serpent, all representing the power of darkness and chaos. Although the allusion is present, the *ruach* is not explicitly placed in opposition to these forces, but rather has the

---

[31] Eichrodt, *Theology*, II, p. 49. Eichrodt also says that the joining of the word with the spirit prevents spirit possession from degenerating into magic or thaumaturgy because the presence of the word prevents the subjecting of the spirit to human control or will (cf. also p. 29).

[32] Cf. Gustav Hölscher, *Das Buch Hiob* (Handbuch zum Alten Testament; Tübingen: J.C.B. Mohr (P. Siebeck), 1952), p. 65. N.H. Tur-Sinai, *The Book of Job: A New Commentary* (Jerusalem: Kiryath Sepher, 1957), pp. 383-84, with a different word division, has read v. 13a: 'By his wind he put the sea into a net', but the different translation does not change the basic meaning of *ruach*.

[33] Cf. Terrien, *Job* (IB), p. 1094, 'a poetic description of *creatio ex nihilo* … the motifs of pagan dualism are absorbed within the overwhelming monism of the theologian'. For the interpretation of *ruach* here as the spirit of God, cf. Terrien, *Job* (Neuchâtel: Delachaux and Niestlé, 1963), p. 217, n. 4.

subordinate role of clearing the field of battle. The *ruach* is the creative and life-giving power of God which brings forth light from darkness.

(d) Psalm 104.30 speaks of the spirit as the creative power of God which brings into being and maintains the life of all creatures:

> 29 When thou hidest thy face, they are dismayed:
>> when thou takest away their breath (רוחם) they die
>> and return to their dust.
> 30 When thou sendest forth thy Spirit (תשלח רוחך)
>> they are created;
>> and thou renewest the face of the ground.

On the one hand, the mention of the life-giving spirit has reference to the divine in-breathing of Gen. 2.7. On the other hand, the use of יבראון ('created'), recalls Gen. 1.1-2, where the divine creative act was mediated solely through the sending forth of the spirit.

It should be noted that 'their breath' in v. 29 is related to 'thy spirit' in v. 30 by the fact of their juxtaposition and the similarity in terminology (*ruach*). But that they are not identical, and that the Psalmist meant to distinguish the two, seems clearly indicated by the modifying pronouns, 'their' breath and 'thy' spirit. The distinction made between the life-breath in humans and the unique life-giving spirit of God seems to be substantiated by this verse. In carefully distinguishing the creative spirit of God from the life-breath in the nostril of every creature, the Psalmist has precluded that concept of the spirit of God which would make of it a substance or a life force which emanates throughout the universe and exists in the nostrils of all creatures. Such a concept would make every creature the possessor of a portion of the divine and would contradict the strict separation between God and his creation which the Old Testament so frequently and so vividly describes.

Nonetheless, the 'breath' in humans is related to the person of God and to his spirit by the very fact that human breath as a symbol of life is created by God. In this sense it belongs to God[34] and can be taken away according to his discretion, a fact which is clearly expressed in v. 29. Human breath is always at the disposition of God's grace and must continually be renewed by a creative act of

---

[34] And it is in this sense that Gen. 6.3, Num. 16.22, 27.16, and Job 27.3 use it.

grace. In describing this creative act, v. 30 hints at the divine in-breathing of Gen. 2.7 through its use of *ruach,* readily translatable as 'breath'. But it stops short of identifying the divine breath of v. 30 with the human breath mentioned in v. 29,[35] choosing rather to describe the creation in terms of a divine fiat, 'they are created'. This conclusion places this passage much closer to Gen. 1.1-3 than to Gen. 2.7.

God's creative power is thought of metaphorically and anthro-pomorphically as his breath, suggested by the word *ruach.* But it is this life-creating power which is also known to men as God's spirit, also suggested by the word *ruach.* Verses 29-30 express clearly the truth that life-potential exists only in God. Humanity only lives as a recipient.

Verse 30, judging from the context in vv. 10-28, has reference to the continuing creation and not to the original creation. Verses 17-23 also show that animals as well as men are included.

2. Humanity's Creator: God's Inbreathing

Psalm 104.30 provides the transition from cosmic creation to the creation of human life, for in this verse the Psalmist describes the creation of all breathing life. Job 34.14-15, strikingly similar to Ps. 104.30, narrows the focus to humans, 'If he should take back his spirit to himself, and gather to himself his breath, all flesh would perish together, and man would return to the dust'.

Finally, Elihu in Job 33.4 individualizes the creative work of the spirit in a verse whose second line appears to have direct reference to Gen. 2.7, 'The spirit of God has made me and the breath of the Almighty gives me life'. The poet in this verse is interpreting Gen. 2.7 in terms of creation by the spirit of God.

3. Regeneration as New Creation

Whenever God gives life to the dead there is a creation. This can take place, according to the biblical writers, in the natural world, in the nation Israel, or in the individual heart. In the time of the exile when the body of Israel appeared totally dead, the prophets saw at work the creative power of Yahweh giving new life to his people. Three great exilic texts considered this to be the work of the spirit,

---

[35] Just as Gen. 2.7 does by its avoidance of the term '*ruach*', Yahweh breathes into him and he becomes alive.

the means by which Yahweh breathed new life into his land and people: Ezek. 37.14, Isa. 32.15, and Isa. 44.3.

In the first of these contexts, Ezekiel is brought in a vision to a valley full of bones. Ezekiel is commanded by the Lord to prophesy 'to the breath' in order that it will come and make the dry bones alive again. As Ezekiel obeys, the breath comes into the bones and they become alive. As the vision ends, Yahweh explains its meaning. 'I will open your graves, and raise you from your graves, O my people; and I will bring you home into the land of Israel' (v. 12). Verse 14 continues, 'And I will put my Spirit within you, and you shall live (ונתתי רוחי בכם וחייתם) and I will place you in your own land ...' The passage speaks about the resurrection of the nation. Israel in exile is a dead corporate body because the people are separated from Yahweh, the only source of life (cf. v. 11, 'we are clean cut off'). But just as Yahweh through his life-giving spirit breathed life into the inert clay and called into life the first human, so now he can, through the same spirit, revive the corporate body of the people Israel and return them to their own land. Verses 1 to 10,[36] in an obvious reference to Gen. 2.7, describe figuratively by means of a vision the reality that is explained in vv. 11-14. The author of the 'breath' in vv. 9-10 is introduced in v. 14. It is the spirit of Yahweh which gives life and which likewise can also restore life to that which is dead.

Isaiah 32.15 describes a regeneration of the land as well as the nation:

15 until the Spirit is poured out on us from on high,
(עד-יערה עלינו רוח ממרום)
   and the wilderness becomes a fruitful field,
   and the fruitful field is deemed a forest.
16 Then justice will dwell in the wilderness,
   and righteousness abide in the fruitful field.
17 And the effect of righteousness will be peace.
   and the result of righteousness, quietness and trust forever.

---

[36] The *ruach* in vv. 9-10 is the breath in every creature, symbolic of life. But breath does not make alive, especially breath coming from the four winds (the breath, or life, of Israel is to come from the four winds because it was scattered to the four winds, cf. 5.10-12). Only God makes alive. So vv. 9-10 explain the enlivening *process* whose *author* ('my spirit') is described in v. 14. The spirit of God is not described in vv. 9-10, only the human breath.

Verses 15-20 have no apparent connection to v. 14 and the immediately preceding section. But the passage should probably be
considered a continuation of the description of the future age described in vv. 1-5, a description which has been interrupted by the
denunciation of existing evils (vv. 6-14). The section consisting of
vv. 15-20 neatly ties together both vv. 1-5 and vv. 6-14. The era of
the king ruling in righteousness and justice (v. 1) will coincide with
the giving of the spirit and the resulting reign of righteousness and
justice (vv. 15-17). This will serve to correct the existing injustices
denounced in vv. 6 and 7. The fruitful field and the miraculous re-
juvenation of nature will be the reversal of the poor harvests and
neglected fields of vv. 10 and 13. These calamities have come on
the nation as punishment for social crimes, oppression, and unbe-
lieving complacency. The nation abiding 'in a peaceful habitation, in
secure dwellings, and in quiet resting places' (v. 18) is a direct response to the judgment pronounced on Jerusalem, 'the joyful city',
in v. 14.

The spirit of God, as the only giver of life, bestows new life in
every realm after the destruction and death spoken of in 32.9-14.
Destruction comes 'in little more than a year' (v. 10); the renewal
coming from the pouring out of the spirit is placed in the indefinite
future.

Nature is to be renewed. This represents not just an increase in
fertility but a transformation from a wilderness to a fertile field. Just
as all of creation received the gift of life from God through the
spirit in the beginning, and just as nature must suffer along with
humanity because of humanity's sin (vv. 10-14), so nature again will
share in the renewal of creation which comes with the pouring out
of the spirit. It will not be limited to a 'spiritual' renewal. Nevertheless, the emphasis in this passage is on the renewal of the nation,
'poured upon *US*'. The results of the renewal of the society of Israel will be justice, righteousness, peace, quietness, and trust forever.
It is the return of paradise.

It should be noted that 'physical' life and spiritual life are not
strictly distinguished here. The spirit of God as the giver of life
gives physical and spiritual renewal blended together. This is particularly noticeable in v. 16 where there is joined justice and wilderness, righteousness and a fertile field. Genesis 3, in portraying the
consequences of the fall, has the same blending of the 'physical'

and the 'spiritual'. This passage shows that the new life inspired by the spirit cannot be sharply divided into the categories 'physical' and 'spiritual' or 'man' and 'nature'. All life comes from the spirit.

This second creation, the bestowal of a new life, can only come when the spirit is 'poured out'. The verb is not meant to indicate the nature of the spirit, as if it were a substance like water, for the suffering servant 'poured out his soul to death' (Isa. 53.12). It only means that the spirit is given in its fullness and in great abundance as if God emptied out his inexhaustible power on the nation. The ways between God and his people will be opened wide.

Isaiah 44.3-5 extends to the gentiles the gift of life through the spirit usually reserved for Israel alone.

> 3   For I will pour water on the thirsty land,
>   and streams on the dry ground;
>   I will pour my Spirit upon your descendants,
>   (אצק רוחי על־זרעך)
>   and my blessing on your off-spring.
> 4   They shall spring up like grass amid waters,
>   like willows by flowing streams.
> 5   This one will say, 'I am the Lord's',
>   another will call himself by the name of Jacob …

The promise is given for the new age that the work of the Servant (vv. 1, 2) will be aided by the spirit, poured out as a life-giving stream on the parched and desolate hearts, not only of the physical sons of Israel who had turned away from Yahweh, but also on non-Israelites. Here for the first time is described the regeneration by the spirit of God of both Israelites and non-Israelites. If only Israelites are meant, there would be no purpose in their taking the name Jacob.[37] The regeneration is thoroughgoing, the vision is universal.

B. Yahweh's Presence in the Spirit

To behold the face of Yahweh, that is to say, to be in his presence and commune with him was the privilege and everlasting delight of his people. Thus when Yahweh hid his face, he was angry and punishment would result. Israel experienced the lash of Yahweh's displeasure in the exile. Ezekiel expressed this in terms of the with-

---

[37] Cf. James Muilenburg, *Isaiah*, in G.A. Buttrick (ed.), The Interpreter's Bible (New York: Abingdon-Cokesbury Press, 1956), p. 503.

drawal of Yahweh's presence: 'And the nations shall know that the house of Israel went into captivity for their iniquity, because they dealt so treacherously with me that I hid my face from them and gave them into the hand of their adversaries ...' (39.24).

But this was not to be Yahweh's final word. Just as Ezekiel 37 promised the restoration of the nation through the enlivening power of the spirit, so 39.29 promised further the gift of Yahweh's presence with his people to be realized through the spirit: 'I will not hide my face any more from them, when I pour out my Spirit upon the house of Israel, says the Lord God'.

This use of spirit to signify the presence of God is extremely unusual. It was not encountered in the earlier periods and appears for the first time in the exilic period. Previously, *ruach* could refer to Yahweh's power, his mind, or his will; that is, to particular aspects of his being. Here it refers to the fullness of his being, his presence. God himself is present with his people in his spirit.

Only one other text in the Old Testament period uses the spirit of God with the meaning of presence: Ps. 139.7, 'Whither shall I go from thy Spirit? Or whither shall I flee from thy presence?' This Psalm does not describe the presence of Yahweh with the nation. As vv. 8-10 show, this is the universal (or continual) presence of Yahweh with the individual believer. This also could not refer to the cultic presence of Yahweh, still a possibility for Ezek. 39.29. It is completely individual and completely universal. There is not the slightest hint of a cultic presence geographically fixed in Jerusalem.

The destruction of Jerusalem and the exiling of large segments of the worshiping congregation served to break down the religious exclusivism which tended to develop around Jerusalem and the temple.[38] It changed the notion that Yahweh could only be approached for worship in Jerusalem. The exile made more possible the highly individual, widely universal type of song represented by Psalm 139. It became possible for a human being to declare, as did this psalmist, that Yahweh's presence could accompany the believer wherever in the world s/he might be. It was through the spirit that Yahweh could continually be present with his children.

---

[38] For a text which shows that an earlier period considered it necessary to be in Israel in order to enjoy Yahweh's presence, cf. 1 Sam. 26.19-20.

5

'EVEN UPON YOUR SLAVES': EXILE AND EARLY RECONSTRUCTION, CONTINUED

I. The Woof: Persistence of Earlier Strands

Exilic influence on the spirit concept is seen not so much in the appearance of a great variety of new forms of the spirit, but in the reappearance, in great number and with evident changes, of earlier categories. The texts from this period, however, are not mere duplicates of earlier periods. There are obvious and significant changes pointing to a growth in the spirit concept.

A. Prophetic Spirit

(a) Some texts from this period, however, do repeat old forms with little variation, for example, Isa. 48.16 or 61.1; or are merely a memory of earlier days, Zech. 7.12. Then there is Joel 3.1-2 (RSV 2.28-29), a text that is most characteristic of all that is new and different in this period.

> 1 And it shall come to pass afterward,
> > that I will pour out my spirit on all flesh;
> > > (אשפוך את־רוחי על־כל־בשר)
> > Your sons and your daughters shall prophesy,
> > > your old men shall dream dreams,
> > and your young men shall see visions.
> 2 Even upon the menservants and maidservants
> > in those days, I will pour out my spirit.

These two verses stand as an independent unit in the immediate context. Whether they are considered to be part of the one section 2.18-4.21 (RSV 2.18-3.21), interpreted as the oracle of Yahweh given in response to the plea and repentance of the congregation, or whether they are considered to be part of the section 3.1-4.21 (RSV 2.28-3.21), which describes the signs of the day of the Lord, it must be observed that they are joined only loosely to what immediately precedes (v. 27 has the sound of a conclusion) and not at all to what follows. If this is true, it means that the interpreter of these verses cannot draw on the context for their interpretation.

'Afterward' (אחרי־כן) is a formula of transition which can either mean 'next' or 'later on'. The word does not necessarily point to the distant future or to the eschaton, but it does point forward to something that has not yet taken place.

The verb 'pour out' ranges this verse alongside Isa. 32.15 (יערה), Isa. 44.3 (אצק), and Ezek. 39.29 (שפכתי) in anticipating a day in the future when God's spirit will be sent not by measure but in inexhaustible abundance. It might be noted that, as in Isa. 32.15, 44.3, and Ezek. 36.27-30, it is joined to a renewal in nature (2.23-27), although in this case the renewal precedes rather than follows the giving of the spirit.

According to Joel, all Israel is to receive the spirit:[1] sons and daughters, old men and young men, slaves and women.[2] In other words, it is not limited to the 'old men', the elders (Numbers 11), or even to 'men', the elders, judges, leaders; but it included young men, women and daughters.

The reference of this passage is to Moses' wish (Num. 11.29) that all God's people might be prophets, that God would give his spirit to all of them. This may be the reason for the use of the word

---

[1] But limited to Israel in spite of the phrase 'all flesh'. For this phrase is qualified by 'your' sons and daughters, 'your' old men, etc., cf. J.A. Thompson, *Joel* IB, Vol. VI, p. 752, and many others. This is how this passage was interpreted on Pentecost. Otherwise, there would not have been the great astonishment when it was poured out also on Cornelius (Acts 10.45).

[2] C.F. Keil, *The Twelve Minor Prophets* Vol. I (Grand Rapids: Eerdmans 1949), pp. 211-12, says, 'the outpouring of the Spirit upon slaves (men-servants and maidens) is connected by *vegam*, as being something very extraordinary, and under existing circumstances not to be expected. Not a single case occurs in the whole of the Old Testament of a slave receiving the gift of prophecy ... And the communication of this gift was irreconcilable with the position of slaves under the Old Testament. Consequently even the Jewish expositors could not reconcile themselves to this announcement. The LXX by rendering it ἐπὶ τοὺς δούλους μου καὶ ἐπὶ τὰς δούλας μου, have put servants of God in the place of slaves of men; and the Pharisees refused to the ὄχλος even knowledge of the law (Jn 7.49)'.

'prophesy'. 'Prophesying' was the phenomenon that was present when the spirit was given to the elders. Dreams and visions are mentioned as media of prophetic revelation in Num. 12.6 (cf. also 1 Kgs 22.19 and Amos 7.1-9).

What effects of the coming of the spirit did the prophet Joel envision when he referred to prophesying, dreams, and visions? Is it the ecstatic state suggested by the reference to Numbers 11?[3] This, however, is not credible in view of the disfavor into which this ecstatic 'prophesying' had fallen. It has also been proposed that the effect of the spirit as described by Joel will be 'a new relation to God'.[4] This interpretation depends on the joining of 2.27 to 3.1 as if they together said what is stated in Ezek. 39.29: that God will be in the midst of Israel, that he will truly be present to all in Israel when he pours out his spirit on them. But 2.27 and 3.1 are joined too loosely to give this interpretation, being actually separated by the transition phrase rather than joined.

It is preferable to see in Joel a reference to legitimate revelation media (Num. 12.6) as though the prophet were saying that all in Israel are now to become prophets in the manner of the great, traditional prophets. All are to hear God's word directly through the spirit without having to receive it through the mediation of specially appointed 'prophets'. And all will proclaim it, witnessing to the saving acts of the God that they now know through his spirit.

The spirit in Joel is the true prophetic spirit revealing God's word to all in Israel. Whether this nation of prophets is now to witness to the nations[5] cannot be determined from the text.

(b) Isaiah 59.21 resembles Joel 3.1-2 in the fact that the gift of the spirit is enlarged to include all in Israel:

20 'And he will come to Zion as Redeemer,
    to those in Jacob who turn from transgression,'
says the Lord.

---

[3] Thus Kapelrud, *Joel Studies* (Uppsala: Almqvist Wiksells, 1948), p. 133, who has confused the *niph'al* of נבא which was only used of the legitimate prophetic vocation in Israel's early days, with the *hithpa'el,* which was used to designate the ecstatic condition or 'raving'. It is the *niph'al* that is used here in 3.1.

[4] Cf. H.W. Wolff, *Joel,* (BK, Neukirchen: Neukirchener Verlag, 1963), pp. 78-79, who denies that Joel is anticipating a nation of ecstatics or of prophets proclaiming God's oracles.

[5] Cf. Lys, *Ruach, le Souffle dans l'Ancien Testament*, p. 249.

21 'And as for me, this is my covenant with them, says the Lord:
My spirit which is upon you (רוחי אשר עליך),
and my words which I have put in your mouth,
shall not depart out of your mouth,
or out of the mouth of your children, says the Lord,
from this time forth and for evermore'.

'My words' are not the law (cf. Exod. 19.7, 8; 20.1; Deut. 30.14), which is never spoken of in the Old Testament as inspired by the spirit, and never associated directly with the spirit. Rather, 'my words' indicates God's revelation communicated through his word, which has been placed in the mouth of the servant, Israel (cf. 51.16). Although not expressly so stated, the mention of the spirit in this context indicates that the word placed in the mouth of the individual believer in Israel is inspired by the spirit. The word which hitherto has been in the mouth of the prophets will henceforth not be restricted to select individuals. The covenant is not a new covenant but the fulfillment of the old, and recalls a similar promise in Hag. 2.4, 5, 'I am with you according to the promise that I made you when you came out of Egypt. My Spirit abides among you ...' The spirit, however, should not be separated from the word. It is the spirit given to the servant (cf. 42.1) which will enable him to perform his prophetic task. It is the servant, Israel, that is also addressed in 59.21, to whom the spirit and the words of God have already been granted. God's revelation through the spirit, and the word he inspires is the realization of the covenant promise. It is the presence of his spirit which gives the assurance that the salvation proclaimed in v. 20 is not long in coming.[6]

(c) The function of the spirit in the difficult text Isa. 34.16 is not easy to establish.[7] The whole chapter deals, in apocalyptic terms, with the destruction of Edom and the subsequent population of the desolated land (*tohu* and *bohu* in v. 11) with a varied assortment of animals usually found in wild or desolate country. The part played by the spirit in this weird drama is explained in v. 16:

[6] Cf. Muilenburg, *Isaiah*, p. 696.
[7] Few commentators comment directly on the meaning of *ruach* in this post-exilic text. Some speak of it obliquely in terms of Yahweh's controlling purpose, cf. James Muilenburg, 'The Literary Character of Isaiah 34', *JBL* 59.3 (1940), p. 356. Delitzsch, *Isaiah,* p. 75, relates it to the mouth of Yahweh as 'breath' to the creative word.

Seek and read from the book of the Lord:
>   Not one of these shall be missing;
>   none shall be without her mate.
For the mouth of the Lord has commanded,
>   and his Spirit has gathered them (ורוחו הוא קבצן)

There is an allusion to Sodom and Gomorrah in vv. 9-10, and to
Noah's ark in the above verse, 'none … without her mate'. But that
is no aid in defining the role of the spirit; which played no part in
any of the early Genesis narratives. Another explanation could be:
just as the animals were preserved in the ark to re-inhabit the earth
after the flood, so Yahweh, through word and spirit, preserves the
animals to re-inhabit desolated Edom after her complete destruction. Muilenburg's description of this chapter as the 'undoing of
creation'[8] is particularly suggestive here. It could be thought that
just as the spirit and the word were active in creation, so they are
also active at the 'undoing of creation'.

It seems better, however, to relate the spirit and the word to the
book of the Lord, the prophetic word. The reference could be to
the book of Isaiah's prophecies.[9] Mouth and spirit seem to stand in
a parallel construction, meaning that the *command* of the mouth of
Yahweh and the *gathering* done by the spirit are not separate actions
but a rephrased statement of the same action. The command of the
mouth of the Lord, if it is not to be left dangling, will have to be
joined to the 'book of the Lord'. It is in the book of the Lord that
this command to gather certain animals has been written, presumably by the prophet Isaiah. It was the spirit that inspired in the
prophet Yahweh's word of command, designating the animals to be
gathered. However, it may also be that *ruach* is the breath by which
the word of command written in the book of prophecy is uttered.
If this is the meaning of *ruach,* then the relation between *ruach* and
word is the contrary of that in Gen. 1.2. Here it is the breath which
gives expression to the word, incarnates it, and executes it. The
ruach does not leave the command 'hanging in the air' but puts it
into action.[10] The *ruach* here is the prophetic spirit related to the
prophetic word.

---

[8] Muilenburg, 'The Literary Character of Isaiah 34', p. 345.
[9] Cf. Delitzsch, *Isaiah*, p. 75; Fohrer, *Das Buch Jesaja*, p. 145.
[10] Cf. Lys, *Ruach, le Souffle dans l'Ancien Testament*, p. 219.

B. Charisma

(a) In the case of the servant (Isa. 42.1) as with the messianic king (Isa. 11.2), it is the endowment with the spirit of God that will equip him for his mission. In this respect there is in this verse a continuation of that charismatic work of the spirit seen even in the earliest period.

1 Behold my servant, whom I uphold,
      my chosen, in whom my soul delights;
   I have put my spirit upon him (נתתי רוחי אליו),
      he will bring forth justice to the nations.
2 He will not cry or lift up his voice,
      or make it heard in the street ...

The servant, through the spirit, receives the charisma which enables him to accomplish his task, a task which in most respects is prophetic. It is pastoral (vv. 3a, b). But it is also kerygmatic, the universal proclamation of *mishpat*[11] (vv. 1, 3, 4), the Yahwistic faith, the belief in the true God. As a prophet, the servant appears to be modeled after Moses in Num. 11.17, who was endowed with the spirit and as such was considered to be a prophet (v. 29). And as the Torah was mediated through Moses, so the new *torah* will be mediated through the servant (v. 4b). As Moses mediated the covenant and led his people out of bondage, so the servant is the mediator of a new covenant to the nations, whom he will lead out of bondage (vv. 7-8).[12] But unlike the early ecstatic *nebiim,* whose violent conduct under the influence of the spirit came into disrepute, the servant 'will not cry or lift up his voice, or make it heard in the street'.[13] That is to say, the *spirit* will make him a loving and gentle pastor of those who are placed in his care. In this text the spirit of Yahweh is the gift-bestowing spirit which both inspires the message of the servant, and makes him a person who can bring the nations to know the true God.[14]

---

[11] J. Smart, *History and Theology in Second Isaiah* (Philadelphia: Westminster 1965), p. 83, says that *mishpat* is parallel 'to what in the New Testament is called the Kingdom of God'.

[12] Cf. Koch, *Geist und Messias,* pp. 108-10, and von Rad, *Old Testament Theology* (London: Oliver & Boyd, 1962), II, p. 273.

[13] Cf. Paul Volz, *Der Geist Gottes* (Tübingen: J.C.B. Mohr, 1910), p. 98.

[14] C.A. Briggs, 'The Use of רוח in the Old Testament', *JBL* XIX (1900), pp.

(b) There are three texts from the Priestly source which present the charismatic function of the spirit in a drastically altered form. No longer is the charismatic designation limited to those chosen to be Israel's leaders. The technical skills of tailors and artisans are now considered to be the charisma of the spirit. These skills are pressed into service in the manufacture of cult objects.

In the interpretation of these texts it is necessary that they be considered together, for the interpretation of the latter, Exod. 31.3, 35.31, aids in the interpretation of the former. Exodus 28.3 speaks of those who are to make Aaron's garments, showing that they are to be given the ability to do the work well. The verse reads: 'and you shall speak to all who have ability (חכמי לב), whom I have endowed with an able mind (מלאתיו רוח חכמה), that they make Aaron's garments to consecrate him for my priesthood'. Exodus 31.2-4 is more explicit in describing the ability given to Bezalel to make the furnishings for the tabernacle:

> The Lord said to Moses, See, I have called by name Bezalel the son of Uri, son of Hur, of the tribes of Judah: and I have filled him with the Spirit of God (ואמלא אתו רוח אלהים), with ability (חכמה) and intelligence, with knowledge and all craftsmanship, to devise artistic design to work in gold, silver, and bronze ...

Exod. 35.31 relates the fact that Moses relayed the Lord's words of Exodus 31.1-11 to the people. The formula is identical with 31.3.

In Exod. 28.3 the *ruach* is called רוח חכמה. On the one hand, it cannot simply be assumed that this refers to the spirit of God, although the *ruach* is called the רוח אלהים in 31.3 and 35.31 in a similar context. On the other hand, 31.3 and 35.31 speak of the gift of the spirit to Bezalel for woodworking and stone cutting, while the *ruach hokhmah* of 28.3 is given to those who are to do the tailoring on the priestly garments. One of these is named in 31.6 (35.34) as Oholiab, who is to be given ability identified in 31.6 as *hokhmah*, 'wisdom' or 'skill'. The *ruach* of 28.3, then, could be interpreted to mean the human *ruach*, evident in this case as the artistic ability which Oholiab possesses. This is not to deny that it is an ability which is ultimately divinely inspired, as the RSV makes clear, 'and I

142-43, sees a reference in this passage to the ancient 'heroic leaders of Israel', (the judges?) in terms of 'executive and administrative power'.

have given to all able men ability'. Two things, however, speak against the interpretation of *ruach* in 28.3 as the human *ruach*. First the *ruach* in humans is used to mean 'disposition', 'will', even 'moral character', but is nowhere in the Old Testament used to refer to ability or talent. Secondly, the human seat of this divinely given ability is consistently referred to as the heart throughout these chapters, (cf. 28.3, 31.6, 35.35, 36.1, 2). God's spirit could be said to be in the human heart but not the human spirit. *Ruach,* then, even in 28.3, must be taken to mean the spirit of God, the divine source of that ability which is now to be placed in the service of the Lord for the construction of the tabernacle and the making of the priestly garments. This God-given charismatic talent is defined as *hokhmah* (or understanding and knowledge) in 28.3, 31.3, 6, 35.31, 35, 36.1, 2; the overall 'wisdom' classification of the various talents displayed in the preparation of the cultic furniture and garments.[15]

It is the gift-giving function of the spirit of God that is described in these three passages. 'The erection of the tabernacle could not have been a human piece of work – the Spirit of God had directly authorized the chief craftsman to undertake the task'.[16] Just as God's 'craftsmanship' at creation (Gen. 2.2, 3; מלאכה) was executed through the spirit, so the 'craftsmanship' (מלאכה) involved in constructing the tabernacle and tailoring the priestly garments is actually the work of God, performed through his spirit by certain select individuals.

The 'wisdom' element is unmistakable and recalls the Joseph narrative (Gen. 41.38).

(c) The other two spirit texts from the Priestly source are a return to the charismatic designation of leadership. Numbers 27.18, which speaks of Joshua as 'a man in whom is spirit', must be taken together with Deut. 34.9. In the former, Yahweh tells Moses, 'Take Joshua the son of Nun, a man in whom is the spirit (אשר רוח בו), and lay your hand upon him'. But the latter text reverses the order

---

[15] McKane, *Prophets and Wise Men,* p. 16, comments on this passage, 'The second point which I would make in connection with these passages is that in Exod. 28.3 the skill of the craftsman is not portrayed in terms of native endowment; it is not the result of a period of rigorous apprenticeship, but is rather the gift of Yahweh who has filled the *hakeme leb* with the spirit (*ruach*) of wisdom. This represents one aspect of the accommodation of the vocabulary of old wisdom to Israelite piety'.

[16] von Rad, *Old Testament Theology,* I, p. 100.

of the ordination and the gift of the spirit: 'And Joshua the son of Nun was full of the spirit of wisdom, for Moses had laid his hands upon him'. Joshua is provided with the divine charisma which means the ability and insight necessary to carry out his assigned task. Because 27.13 does not speak of his receiving the spirit but assumes that Joshua already possesses it, one may conclude that the biblical writer considered Joshua to be one of the seventy elders in Num. 11.25 who had received the spirit (cf. Num. 11.28).

(d) Job 32.8 also offers a significant variation on the theme of the charismatic spirit. Here, not the talents of a leader but rather the wisdom of the sage is the gift of the spirit. There is here and in Exod. 28.3, 31.3, 35.31 a kind of democratization of those gifts of the spirit which hitherto had been reserved for the chosen few. The verse reads: 'But it is the spirit in a man (רוח היא באנוש), the breath of the Almighty that makes him understand (נשמת שדי תבינם)'. Elihu asserts that wisdom is a gift of the spirit of God. The three friends have finished their speeches and Elihu, in deference to their years, has waited in silence until they were finished. But then he declares that, as evidenced by what they have said, it is not merely age which teaches wisdom. It is a special gift of the spirit,[17] the 'breath' of God, which he implicitly claims to have received. It is this wisdom, inspired by God, which he now is anxious to put into words (v. 18). The joining of wisdom and the spirit and the similarities to Gen. 41.38 and Isa. 11.2 should be noted.

---

[17] That a special gift of the spirit of God is meant here, and not the spirit of life in every man, seems indicated by the logic of Elihu's argument. He says that the spirit, not just age, makes one wise. If the spirit of life in man is meant, the human spirit, then the old as well as the young possess it. But Elihu's argument seems to say that the three elders, although aged, have not been granted this spirit, whereas he himself, although much younger, has been specially blessed with the spirit of God which gives wisdom. If the human spirit common to all living creatures is the subject here, there is no meaning in his argument. This would also seem to indicate a difference in meaning between 32.8 and 27.3, where similar phrases are used. Whereas 32.8 speaks of an extraordinary gift of the spirit, 27.3 speaks of the spirit as life or breath in every creature, in other words, the human spirit. However, 27.3 has 'my breath' in parallel with spirit of God, while 32.8, together with 33.4 and 34.14 has 'breath of the Almighty' or 'his breath'. Perhaps the meaning of the spirit, whether it is to be understood as the human spirit or as the unique spirit of God, has been consciously indicated by the writer by his use of 'breath'. Those who interpret *ruach* here as the spirit of God include Terrien, *Job* (IB), p. 1131, who refers to the translations of the Targum and Symmachus for substantiation, and von Rad, *Theology* I, p. 101.

C. Yahweh's Guiding Will

Antecedents for this function of the spirit appear to lie in an earlier period, in Isa. 30.1 and in the Elijah texts: 1 Kgs 18.12, 2 Kgs 2.16. The first text refers more to Yahweh's subjective will, the purpose he had in mind for Israel, while the latter texts describe Yahweh's will as an objective power ruling and directing the activity of the prophet Elijah. Yahweh's will is expressed in these three texts by the word 'spirit'.

(a) The divine will which sought to lead and direct Israel is portrayed most vividly in Isa. 63.7-14, in a hymn to the saving acts of Yahweh. This hymn is contained in the larger community lament of 63.7-64.11. After vv. 8-9, which tell in a general way of Yahweh's care and concern for his people through the course of their history ('carried them all the days of old'), vv. 10-14 continue:

> 10 But they rebelled
>> and grieved his holy spirit (וֹעַצְּבוּ אֶת־רוּחַ קָדְשׁוֹ),
> therefore he turned to be their enemy,
>> and himself fought against them.
> 11 Then he remembered the days of old,
>> of Moses his servant.
> Where is he who brought up out of the sea
>> the shepherds of his flock?
> Where is he who put in the midst of them
>> his holy Spirit (רוּחַ קָדְשׁוֹ),
> 12 who caused his glorious arm
>> to go at the right hand of Moses,
> who divided the waters before them
>> to make for himself an everlasting name,
> 13 who led them through the depths?
>> Like a horse in the desert,
> they did not stumble.
> 14 Like cattle that go down into the valley,
>> the Spirit of the Lord gave them rest (רוּחַ יְהוָה תְּנִיחֶנּוּ).
> So thou didst lead they people,
>> to make for thyself a glorious name.

Verse 10 speaks about the exile, because v. 11 states that 'he remembered the days of old', seemingly far removed in time from the action of v. 10. In the shock of the exile, Israel remembered the old narratives, how Yahweh brought Israel through the sea, equipped its leaders with the spirit, led the people through the desert and settled them, again by the guidance of the holy spirit, in Canaan. All of this is recalled at a time when the guidance of the spirit is no longer experienced, when God is no longer present through his spirit to aid and succor his people during the dark days of the exile.

The translation of v. 10 should be, 'But they rebelled and resisted his holy spirit'.[18] The spirit in this verse does not mean emotion or disposition but rather will. Israel rebelled and resisted Yahweh's holy will, the guidance Yahweh offered her throughout her history (cf. v. 9).

Spirit in v. 11b is usually interpreted as referring to the event in Num. 11.17-29, the spirit given to Moses or the elders or both. In the original passage, Num. 11.17-29, the spirit was the charismatic spirit. Here it represents Yahweh's guidance and loving care for his people. So *ruach* in v. 11 has essentially the same meaning as in v. 10.

Verse 14b has no recognizable allusion to an event or period in Israel's history. It may be a veiled reference to the period of the judges when Israel settled down in Canaan and eventually spread out into the more fertile lowlands. As confirmed by the following line (v. 14c) this settling down process was mediated by Yahweh's spirit working though the judges. Again the meaning of the *ruach* here is Yahweh's guidance. Some commentators[19] propose the emendation of תנחנו for תניחנו giving the meaning of 'led them' rather than 'gave them rest'. This only emphasizes the meaning of Yahweh's guidance found not only in the three occurrences of *ruach* (vv. 10, 11, 14), but also throughout the whole hymn.[20]

Two further comments can be made about the spirit in these verses. First, the spirit does not participate in the struggle against the sea, although it is tempting to see in v. 11e a reference to Exod. 15.8, 10. But the spirit is reserved for action in humanity.[21] It is not even Moses' arm (Exod. 14.21a) but only Yahweh himself who di-

---

[18] See the exegesis of this verse below, Chapter 7, Section IV.
[19] Smart, *History and Theology in Second Isaiah,* p. 269, and Muilenburg, *Isaiah,* p. 735.
[20] Muilenburg, *Isaiah,* p. 735, says, 'The thought of Yahweh's leading dominates this whole section and comes to its splendid culmination in the last two lines'.
[21] Cf. Lys, *Ruach, le Souffle dans l'Ancien Testament,* pp. 155-56.

vides the sea. The spirit is seen to be the means by which, working through his chosen leaders, God led his nation, not only in the early days (vv. 11, 14) but right up to the exile (v. 10).

Secondly, it is called a 'holy spirit'. The spirit partakes of the nature of Yahweh himself. Through use of the term 'holy spirit' the guidance granted to Israel is described in terms of moral purpose. It says as much about the realm of activity of the spirit as about the nature of the spirit itself.

This passage, in describing the function of the spirit as guidance, has clearly shown the element of will in the spirit. And in describing the spirit as 'holy', the prophet has defined an ethical element which has not previously been explicitly present.

In contrast with Yahweh's guidance which Israel resisted in the past, Ezek. 36.27 describes a day in the future when Israel, and each individual in her, will be recreated in such a way that they will be enabled to follow Yahweh's guidance.

> For I will take you from the nations, and gather you from all the countries, and bring you into your own land. I will sprinkle clean water upon you, and you shall be clean from all your uncleannesses, and from all your idols I will cleanse you. A new heart I will give you, and a new spirit I will put within you; and I will take out of your flesh the heart of stone and give you a heart of flesh. And I will put my spirit within you (ואת־רוחי אתן בקרבכם) and cause you to walk in my statutes and be careful to observe my ordinances. You shall dwell in the land which I gave to your fathers; and you shall be my people, and I will be your God (Ezek. 36.24-27).

Through the sprinkling, old weeds are cleared away; then through the creation of a new heart, new ground is provided, and with the giving of the spirit of God, an obedient and fruitful life can spring forth.

This theme of guidance has moved from the external control exerted *on* the person of Elijah, to the *inner* direction that Yahweh had in mind for the nation Israel (Isa. 30.1) to the present text. Ezekiel shows that the giving of the spirit means inner guidance for the ordinary believer. There is also a moral direction expressed which was not explicit in the earlier texts. The text is put into a covenant framework by the formula in v. 28, 'you shall be my people, and I will be your God', and, as is frequently to be seen in covenant renewal contexts, the renewal of nature is included in vv. 29-30.

(c) The progression from forgiveness to regeneration to the new life of obedience in the spirit, so apparent in Ezek. 36, is also evident in Ps. 51.9-14 (RSV 51.7-12). The similarities between the two texts are so pronounced, extending even to the new heart and the new spirit as well as the gift of the spirit of God, that direct dependence can be supposed. The actual function of the spirit of God in Ps. 51.13 (RSV 51.11) is not clearly indicated. Thus the fact that it is paralleled by Ezek. 36.25-27 is of great assistance in its interpretation.

12 Create in me a clean heart, O God,
    and put a new and right spirit within me.
13 Cast me not away from thy presence,
    and take not thy holy Spirit from me.
    (ורוח קדשך אל־תקח ממני)
14 Restore to me the joy of thy salvation,
    and uphold me with a willing spirit.

The development of thought in this well-known penitential psalm is clear. The psalmist calls on Yahweh for mercy, vv. 3-4. He makes his confession of sin in vv. 5-8. Verses 9-11 are a request that Yahweh will forgive the sin which has been confessed. The following section, which is relevant here, contains the psalmist's request for inward renewal (vv. 12-14), followed by the vow of personal dedication (vv. 15-19) and finally an appended prayer for Jerusalem.

In regard to the classification of *ruach* in these three verses, it seems clear, first of all, that *ruach* in v. 12 is the spirit in humanity because it stands in a parallel construction with the heart which is to be created in the psalmist. The spirit of v. 12 is not to be confused with God's spirit in v. 13, which is identified as 'thy' spirit. The classification of spirit in v. 14 is more difficult, and depends on the translation of the accompanying adjective. If נדיבה is to be translated noble or princely, it could refer to God's spirit. But most present-day commentators favor the meaning of 'willing'[22] which

---

[22] Cf. E.R. Dalglish, *Psalm Fifty-One in the Light of Ancient Near Eastern Paternism* (Leiden: F.J. Brill, 1962), p. 162, or Artur Weiser, *The Psalms* (London: SCM Press, 1962), p. 408.

would then make it the psalmist's spirit, the spirit in humanity. The spirit of God would not be described as 'willing'.

It is necessary, then, to determine the meaning and function of *ruach* only in v. 13, and not in v. 12 or v. 14.

The meaning of *ruach* is usually decided by the interpretation given to the first member of the parallel construction in v. 13, 'cast me not away from thy presence'. The presence of Yahweh has been understood in terms of divine fellowship and personal communion with Yahweh himself. The principal objection to this interpretation, however, is that a plea for the non-cessation of fellowship with Yahweh uttered at this point in the psalm interrupts in a very decided way the smooth progression in thought evident in the poem. A plea that one not be cast away from Yahweh's presence, given this interpretation, would be entirely in place when the psalmist is calling on Yahweh for mercy (vv. 3-4), when he is confessing his sin (vv. 5-8), or even when he is asking for forgiveness (vv. 9-11). It is just because of this great burden of unforgiven sin that the psalmist is in critical danger of being excluded entirely from the presence of Yahweh, which will mean the severance of divine fellowship and spiritual death.

But having confessed his sin and having requested Yahweh's forgiveness, the psalmist in v. 12 moves on to the problem of his own inner transformation as if the problem of his past sin had been rightly and finally dealt with by confession and a plea for forgiveness. To return again to sin which has been confessed and forgiven is futile and the psalmist recognizes this by going ahead to the next problem: the necessity of an inner transformation which will preclude another such lapse into sin. Having moved on to the matter of inner renewal, the psalmist will not return to speak now of a severance of fellowship caused by a mortal sin. It is necessary to see in v. 13a a meaning which will carry forward the evident progression in thought developed by the psalmist.

It is proposed, therefore, to understand v. 13a as referring, not to communion with Yahweh, but to his divine guidance. The prototype for this developing pattern of thought which can be seen in vv. 9-13 lies in Ezek. 36.25-27, joined to 39.29. Ezekiel 36.25 speaks of the cleansing from past sins. Verse 26, an almost exact parallel to Ps. 51.12, speaks about the gift of a new heart and a new spirit to the individual members of the nation. Verse 27 speaks of the guidance

Yahweh provides for the individual believer, who will be aided by the spirit and enabled to walk according to the will of Yahweh. Finally, 39.29 equates the spirit of 36.27 with the presence of Yahweh. If Ps. 51.13a is interpreted in this way, after the pattern of Ezek. 36.25-27, as the guiding presence of Yahweh which must not be taken away, then the holy spirit is, as in Ezek. 36.27, the means which Yahweh uses in this guidance.

There is here, then, the clear progression from the forgiveness of past sin, to inner renewal, and to the guidance by Yahweh's spirit which must accompany the new will to be placed in the believer. Verse 14a, to continue the progression, can refer to the joy which comes from forgiveness and inner transformation. Finally, the psalmist, in 14b, asks to be sustained in this new life by being provided with a willing spirit which will make him a cheerful servant of his Lord.

The holy spirit in v. 13b is the spirit of Yahweh given to the believers for the purpose of guiding the believer in his/her walk in obedience to Yahweh's will. There is seen in this psalm the astonishing fact that what has been promised for the future in Ezek. 36.25-27 (or in Jer. 31.31-34), has been considered as actualized in the life of this psalmist!

Finally it should be noted that, unlike Isa. 44.3, and like Ezek. 36.27, v. 12 does not attribute spiritual renewal or conversion to the spirit but to God himself. The spirit is granted to the believer who has already been cleansed and renewed. So, 'holy', it can be said again, defines the realm of the activity of the spirit as much as the nature of the spirit itself. That is to say, because the spirit is holy, 'it cannot abide where there is impurity or rebelliousness'.[23]

(d) Psalm 143.10 states explicitly what was implicit in Ps. 51.13 – 'Teach me to do thy will for thou art my God! Let thy good spirit lead me on a level path'. The spirit is a guide leading the believer to do God's will.

Not all of the texts from this period, however, speak of the spirit in such explicit terms as Yahweh's guiding influence in the moral life of the believer. A large number of spirit texts in Ezekiel take one back directly to the Elijah texts where the spirit was a con-

---

[23] Schoemaker, 'The Use of רוח in the Old Testament and πνεῦμα in the New Testament', p. 28.

trolling power in the prophet's life, expressing at the same time the prophet's subjection to Yahweh's will and the directing power of that will. A few of these Ezekiel texts also speak of the spirit in terms of what might be called Yahweh's subjective will. Yahweh moves as he wills because he alone is Lord. Texts with this latter meaning will be considered first.

(e) Ezekiel 1.12, 20, 21, and 10.17 use *ruach* to designate the motivating impulse of the divine theophanic vehicle having motive power both in the wheels and in the four living creatures. It is stated in 1.12 that 'wherever the spirit would go they [the four living creatures] went (אל־אשר יהיה־שמה הרוח ללכת ילכו), without turning as they went'. Likewise in vv. 20 and 21 it reads:

> Wherever the spirit would go, they went, and the wheels rose along with them; for the spirit of the living creatures (רוח החיה) was in the wheels. When those went, these went; and when those stood, these stood; and when those rose from the earth, the wheels rose along with them; for the spirit of the living creatures was in the wheels.

It should be observed that 'spirit' is masculine and has the article, while the theophanic wind of v. 4 is feminine and lacks the article. The prophet has distinguished the wind of v. 4 from the *ruach* that provides the motive power for the chariot. The RSV translates רוח החיה as 'spirit of the living creatures'. However, the fact that, with the exception of v. 22, 'living creatures' is always in the plural makes this translation suspect. If Ezekiel had meant the spirit of the living creatures, he would have been expected to have used חיות instead of חיה,[24] or at least a plural possessive. It has been argued that he used חיה as a collective singular,[25] but a collective singular only applies in the case of an indefinite number and would not normally be used for 'four creatures'.[26] It is possible that חיה could be a distributive,[27] referring to each creature individually. But for several reasons it seems preferable to translate רוח החיה as 'the

---

[24] Cf. Volz, *Der Geist Gottes*, p. 44.

[25] Cf. C.F. Keil, *The Prophecies of Ezekiel* (Grand Rapids: Eerdmans, 1949), p. 28.

[26] Cf. Volz, *Der Geist Gottes*, p. 44.

[27] Cf. C.A. Cooke, *The Book of Ezekiel* (Cambridge: Cambridge University Press, 1906), p. 27.

spirit of life'.[28] (1) The article and the masculine gender are used for emphasis and indicate more than the ordinary creature spirit. That which is described is rather *The Spirit.* (2) The four living creatures, according to 10.17, are in reality inanimate temple objects (the cherubim) which can in no way provide motive power for the throne chariot. They have as much need as the wheels to be vivified by the spirit.[29] (3) Because Ezekiel shows such great familiarity with the work of the spirit of God elsewhere in his book, it is difficult to believe he would use any spirit other than the spirit of God as the motive power and directing will of a theophany. In other words, it is God's own spirit which is the vivifying power in the theophanic vehicle. The chariot moves according to God's decision.[30] As in Isa. 40.13, the spirit is the volitional center of God's being. It is 'the energizing and directing power of the theophany ...'[31]

(f) The same energizing and directing power of the spirit is indicated in a series of texts beginning with Ezek. 2.2 and ending with 43.5. Here, however, it is the prophet who is under the absolute control of Yahweh's will.

> 2.1-2 And he said to me, 'Son of man, stand upon your feet, and I will speak with you'. And when he spoke to me, the Spirit entered into me and set me upon my feet
> (ותבא בי רוח כאשר דבר אלי ותעמדני על־רגלי)
> and I heard him speaking to me.

> 3.12 Then the Spirit lifted me up ... I heard ...

---

[28] חיים is the usual Old Testament word for life but חיה is used for life in Ezek. 7.13; Job 33.18, 20, 28; Ps. 74.19 and 143.3.

[29] For points one and two and the conclusion reached cf. Lys, *Ruach, le Souffle dans l'Ancien Testament*, p.128.

[30] Cf. H.G. May, *Ezekiel,* in IB, VI, p. 72, and Cooke, *Ezekiel,* p. 12, who prefer the translation 'spirit of the living creatures', but interpret spirit to mean the divine spirit; also C.A. Briggs and E.G. Briggs, *A Critical and Exegetical Commentary on the Book of Psalms* (ICC; Edinburgh: T & T Clark, 1906), II, p. 493, 'divine energy', and Walther Zimmerli, *Ezechiel* (Neukirchen: Neukirchener Verlag, 1963), p. 68, who believes that originally Ezekiel only used הרוה absolutely as in v. 12 to mean the spirit of Yahweh, the throne chariot thus being guided by the will of Yahweh. Through expansion of the text by Ezekiel's disciples, *ruach* came to be qualified by חיה.

[31] Schoemaker, 'The Use of רוח in the Old Testament and πνεῦμα in the New Testament', p. 26.

14   The Spirit lifted me up and took me away, and I went in bitterness in the heat of my spirit, the hand of the Lord being strong upon me; and I came to the exiles at Tel-abib ...

24   But the Spirit entered into me and set me upon my feet ...

8.3   He put forth the form of a hand, and took me by a lock of my head; and the Spirit lifted me up between earth and heaven, and brought me in visions of God to Jerusalem ...

11.1   The Spirit lifted me up, and brought me ...

5   And the Spirit of the Lord fell upon me, and he said to me ...

24   And the Spirit lifted me up and brought me in the vision by the Spirit of God into Chaldea, to the Exiles.

37.1   The hand of the Lord was upon me, and he brought me out by the Spirit of the Lord, and set me down ...

43.5   the Spirit lifted me up, and brought me into the inner court ...

Ruach is consistently feminine and anarthrous. The article and the masculine gender were necessary in 1.12 to distinguish the spirit from the wind of v. 4, and also to identify it as the spirit of God and not of the living creatures. Now that Yahweh has been introduced (1.28), Ezekiel reverts to the usual feminine gender and drops the article as unnecessary for identification.[32] The spirit is a transporting power. The ecstatic condition, if it is such, appears to be brought on by the 'hand' of God (1.3, 3.22, 8.1, 8.3, 33.22, 37.1, 40.1).[33] There is no transporting by the *hand* of God in Ezekiel corresponding to the action of the hand of God upon Elijah (1 Kgs

---

[32] Cf. Lys, *Ruach, le Souffle dans l'Ancien Testament*, p. 130.

[33] For a discussion of the spirit in relation to the hand, mouth, and face of Yahweh, see P. van Imschoot, 'L'Action de l'Esprit de Jahvé dans l'AT', *Revue des Sciences Philosophiques et Theologiques* 23 (1934), p. 587. For a discussion of the hand of God in Ezekiel, cf. Zimmerli, *Ezechiel*, pp. 47-50. For a discussion of the observation that the same activities are often ascribed to both spirit and hand with a listing of pertinent texts, cf. Scheepers, *Die Gees van God en die Gees van die mens in die Oud Testament*, p. 190.

18.46). When Ezekiel writes, 'The hand of the Lord was upon me', he is describing the psychological sensation of receiving a vision, in other words, an ecstatic condition. So the ecstatic condition is not caused by the spirit of Yahweh, but by the hand of Yahweh. Nor does the spirit speak or inspire the word in the prophet.[34] It is always God himself who speaks, as it is stated, 'the word of the Lord came to me'. Neither is the spirit the source of the visions that Ezekiel saw. Although 11.24 does not exclude the possibility that the vision was 'by the Spirit of the Lord', it is more probable that the prophet was 'brought' by the Spirit of God. So the conclusion must be that the spirit does not cause the ecstatic condition, nor does it inspire the prophetic word, but rather, it is the power of God that transported Ezekiel. This is confirmed by the fact that the spirit does not 'fall' upon him (except in 11.5) but 'enters in', 'lifted', 'took', 'brought', and 'set down'. Furthermore, he does not fall down but 'stands up' (2.2); he does not lose consciousness but can hear (3.12). In spite of some similarities, no activity of the spirit related to the ancient *nebiim* is found here.[35]

These differences show that the spirit transporting Ezekiel is the same spirit that was encountered in 1.12, 20, and 21. For the spirit that carries Ezekiel is not a blind motivating power but is purposive. He is carried to Jerusalem to see a vision of God, or to hear the word of the Lord (11.5), or to receive his initial commission (2.3-3.15) It is the volitional and intelligent power of God, and not some dumb force, that moves him. '"Son of man" here, as in Ps 8, designates the weakness of the creature-man and as such, Ezekiel can

---

[34] Westphal, Mylio, 'La Ruach dans l'Ancien Testament'. Bachelor of Theology dissertation (The University of Geneva, Geneva, 1958), p. 75, says that the spirit is the one that speaks to the prophet in Ezek. 11.5, but he has overlooked the fact that the spirit is feminine while the verb 'said' is masculine.

[35] There is no mention in this period of the ecstatic condition associated with the spirit in an earlier period. Perhaps this phenomenon persisted until the time of the exile when, presumably, it died out altogether. The only post-exilic use of the word, 'prophesying', הנבא in the *hithpael,* is, for no obvious reason, to be found in Ezek. 37.10. Otherwise it has disappeared entirely from the vocabulary of the Old Testament after the Elijah narratives (1 Kgs 18.29), except in a few cases in Jeremiah and Ezekiel (13.7), where it is used in a derogatory sense to describe the false prophets, or slanderously, as a third person description of Jeremiah. There is nothing to indicate that Ezekiel's bizarre behavior was in any way related to the ancient 'ecstatic condition'.

94 *The Spirit of God in the Old Testament*

only be enabled to stand before his Lord and receive his commission through the power of the spirit'.[36]

D. Yahweh's Mind
One verse in this period, Isa. 40.13, uses spirit to mean Yahweh's intellect, an extremely unusual connotation for spirit. One other verse in the Old Testament uses spirit with this meaning: Isa. 30.1. In the earlier text there is a mixture of the intellectual, Yahweh planning in his mind what would be best for Israel, with the volitional, Yahweh desiring to have his will obeyed by Israel. But Isa. 40.13-14 pictures Yahweh in cerebration, planning in his spirit the creation of the world.

Some commentators, however, suggest that the LXX erred in its translation of *ruach* as 'mind'.[37] The verse under discussion is part of a larger creation hymn which begins with v. 12. The text, with its Greek translation as quoted by Paul in Rom 11.34 and 1 Cor. 2.16, reads:

12 Who has measured the waters in the hollow of his hand
       and marked off the heavens with a span,
       (מִי מָדַד בְּשָׁעֳלוֹ מַיִם וְשָׁמַיִם בַּזֶּרֶת תִּכֵּן)
   enclosed the dust of the earth in a measure
       and weighed the mountains in scales
       and the hills in a balance?
13 Who has directed the Spirit of the Lord,
       (מִי תִכֵּן אֶת רוּחַ יְהוָה)
       (LXX, τίς γὰρ ἔγνω νοῦν κυρίου)
   or as his counselor has instructed him?
14 Whom did he consult for his enlightenment,
       and who taught him the path of justice,
       and taught him knowledge,
       and showed him the way of understanding?

The interpretation of *ruach* in this passage must be determined by three factors. First, in its obvious reference to the creation narrative of Genesis 1, the spirit must be granted at least the role that it played in Genesis 1. But, second, there are indications that the spirit

---

[36] W. Eichrodt, *Der Prophet Hesekiel, Kapitel 1-18* (Göttingen: Vandenhoeck und Ruprecht, 1959), p. 10.
[37] Muilenburg, *Isaiah*, pp. 436-37.

has been given new emphasis here. That might be shown by the use of the verb תכן. In its *piel* form, as here and in v. 12, it means 'to measure' or 'to regulate'. But the *qal* form of this verb is used three times in the Old Testament, all in the book of Proverbs: 16.2, 21.2, and 24.12. Proverbs 16.2 reads, 'All the ways of a man are pure in his own eyes, but the Lord weighs the spirit (תכן רוחות). Proverbs 21.2 is the same but substitutes 'heart' for 'spirit'. Proverbs 24.12 reads: 'If you say, "Behold, we did not know this"', does not he who weighs the heart perceive it?' 'Weighing the heart' must have reference to the action of the Egyptian god Horus, who weighed the hearts of the dead before Osiris, the judge. When Deutero-Isaiah uses the unusual expression, תכן רוח, he shows familiarity with its use in the wisdom school, where *ruach* and *leb* seem to have been used interchangeably; and, secondly with the Egyptian myth, in which the 'heart' stood for the human will 'weighed' at death to judge its moral condition. It can be concluded that the prophet, whose 'wisdom' characteristics in this passage are pronounced,[38] used the spirit of the Lord to mean more than Yahweh's creative *power,* the meaning of *ruach* which appears in Gen. 1.2. He is pointing to the intelligent center of the being of God himself. The prophet is saying that no one can be in a position to 'judge', to 'weigh', to 'measure' God's spirit, for it is rather Yahweh who, as God and as creator, weighs human hearts.

The fact that spirit in this passage is equivalent to 'heart', in the Old Testament sense of will and intelligence, is confirmed by the third element which determines the meaning of spirit: the immediate context. The series of words 'instructed', 'enlightenment', 'taught', 'knowledge', 'understanding' – all support the meaning of 'mind' for *ruach,* and apparently guided the translator of Isaiah when in the Septuagint he used νοῦν (mind) rather than πνεῦμα for *ruach.* It has been argued that if the prophet meant 'mind', he would have used *leb.*[39] But if he had done so, he would have lost the allusion to Genesis 1 and to the spirit of God as such. The prophet wished to preserve the meaning of spirit that is found in Gen. 1.2 (creative power) but added to it the meanings of intelligence and

---

[38] Muilenburg, *Isaiah,* p. 437, McKane, *Prophets and Wise Men,* p. 243 and others have commented on the wisdom elements in this text.

[39] Muilenburg, *Isaiah,* p. 437.

intellect. The spirit of Yahweh in Isa. 40.13 is the intelligent center of the very being of Yahweh himself, the purposeful power with which he planned and created the world.

E. Yahweh's power

Three texts from the community of the returnees use spirit to mean Yahweh's power at work in the reconstruction of the temple.

In line with his belief that the old covenant is still in force in 520 BCE, Haggai, in 2.5, describes the presence of the spirit in the community of returned exiles as confirmation of the covenant made at Sinai:

> ... work, for I am with you, says the Lord of hosts, according to the promise that I made (אֶת־הַדָּבָר אֲשֶׁר־כָּרַתִּי) you when you came out of Egypt. My Spirit abides among you (עֹמֶדֶת בְּתוֹכְכֶם רוּחִי); fear not (Hag. 2.4b-5).

The prophet is speaking in the name of Yahweh, encouraging the returnees to work on the rebuilding of the temple, an enterprise which seems to have lagged. Innumerable difficulties must be faced and overcome, including poverty (1.6), a shortage of building materials (1.8), and the opposition of hostile neighbors (Ezra 5). But the work must be taken up in the spirit of the ancient tradition of the Holy War ('take courage ... fear not') for Yahweh is in their midst (v. 4), empowering them for the task ahead, and he will provide what is necessary to make the second temple even more glorious than the first (vv. 6-9).

The presence of Yahweh will be realized through his spirit (v. 5b). The difficult grammatical construction of v. 5a, which relates the promise of Yahweh's presence to the Sinaitic covenant, need not be discussed here as it does not affect the meaning of v. 5b. Moreover, there are other indications that the prophet had the Exodus and Sinai in mind when he spoke this oracle. Yahweh's presence with his people is promised in Exod. 33.14 and repeated in Exod. 29.45 (P). As stated above, the ritual of the Holy War ('take courage ... fear not') was often heard during the Conquest, but also in earlier days (Exod. 14.13). There is at least a hint of the 'shaking down' of the Egyptians (Exod. 12.35-36) in v. 6 ('once again ... I will shake all nations') to provide treasures for the temple in the same way that the precious metals and ornaments were once provided for the tabernacle in the wilderness. It is possible that the promise of the spirit here is a reference to the gift of the spirit on Bezalel and his companions, providing them with the skill necessary for work on the tabernacle. But the verb עמדת, 'abides', is used of the pillar of cloud and fire (Exod. 13.21, 14.19, 24) and would recall to the minds of the listeners the presence of Yahweh with his people during the exodus from Egypt and throughout the wilderness wanderings. The use of this word, above all, indicates that the spirit there signifies the continuing personal presence of Yahweh in the midst of this discouraged band of returnees who are laboring to rebuild the temple. His presence means the encouragement and power necessary for the task.

The power of the spirit to finish construction of the temple is also promised in Zech. 4.6.

> Then he said to me, 'this is the word of the Lord to Zerubbabel: Not by power, but by my Spirit (ברוחי) says the Lord of hosts. What are you, O great mountain? Before Zerubbabel you shall become a plain; and he shall bring forth the top stone amid shouts of "Grace, grace to it"' (Zech. 4.6-7).

Verses 6-10a, taken by themselves, present no great difficulty. Yahweh, through his spirit, will furnish the power necessary for the completion of the temple,[40] whose construction is mentioned in vv. 7, 9, and 10. Because he is named four times in as many verses, Zerubbabel must be the one, it is assumed, on whom the power of the spirit will be concentrated. Perhaps the building of the temple has progressed to a certain stage but has been stymied by a mountain of difficulties (Hag. 2.1-9.) At this point the encouragement needed is provided by Zechariah's oracle. The people are to take heart from Yahweh's assurance that his spirit, which far surpasses human talents and power, is at work in their midst. Through the

---

[40] K. Elliger, *Das Buch der zwölf kleinen Propheten* (ATD, Göttingen: Vandenhoeck und Ruprecht, 1951), p. 118, relates the spirit to the completion of the temple but adds that it also means that God himself, through the power of his spirit and not by conventional weapons, will ward off the threat of the Samaritans who seek to disrupt operations. G. von Rad, *Theology*, I, p. 285, sees in this phrase the interpretation that 'Zechariah opposed any idea of bringing in human or political means to defend Jerusalem'. Finally, W.E. Barnes, *Haggai and Zechariah* (Cambridge: Cambridge University Press, 1917), p. 46, says, 'the words are a caution to Zerubbabel not to attempt to restore the kingdom to Judah with the help of the sword'.

power of his spirit the mountain of obstacles will be leveled into a plain and the temple will be completed (vv. 7, 9).

The fact that the people are never mentioned and that Zerubbabel is mentioned so frequently suggests that these verses, in addition to providing encouragement for all those engaged in the task of temple building, are also meant as the divine authentication of the Davidide, Zerubbabel. This provides the clue which will join the vision of vv. 1-5, 10b-14, to the oracle in vv. 6-10a. The oracle seems to be only secondarily joined to the vision. Actually the vision can stand by itself and gives good meaning apart from vv. 6-10a. The only connecting link between the vision and the oracle is the figure of Zerubbabel. It is tempting to interpret the oil, present throughout the vision, as the spirit which flows from the 'two anointed', the 'sons of oil', to the lampstand (vv. 12-14). In this case the 'two anointed' are Zerubbabel and Joshua (6.11), while the lampstand can only represent the congregation of Israel which shines as the eyes of the Lord throughout the whole earth (v. 10a). However, oil is never used in the Old Testament to represent the spirit. Instead, it frequently symbolizes the ritual of anointing, which would suggest that this is its meaning here. It is a well known fact that Zechariah has other 'messianic' references, namely, 3.8-10 and 6.9-14. These probably originally contained the name of Zerubbabel, the son of David (1 Chron. 3.19). Under pressure from the Persian authorities they became the indirect statements which are found in the present book of Zechariah. This suggests that Zech. 4.1-5, 10b-14, also is just such a reference. As the son of David, Zerubbabel is the anointed one, and the oil of grace (Ps. 45.2, 7) flows from him to the nation.

But as the anointed son of David, as a messianic candidate, Zerubbabel can also be expected to have received the gift of the spirit. With a direct reference to 1 Sam. 16.13, by the secondary joining of the vision with the oracle,[41] the prophet can suggest that, just as David, the spirit-filled anointed one, planned the building of the first temple (1 Chron. 22), so now Zerubbabel, the anointed son of David, by the power of the spirit of Yahweh, will be enabled to complete the second temple. This explains why Zerubbabel is mentioned so frequently in verses vv. 6-10a. It is because *he* is the leader

---

[41] Probably by the prophet himself; cf. Weiser, *The Old Testament,* p. 271.

that the success of the temple construction is ensured. The spirit represents the power of Yahweh, but it is to be channeled through the Davidide, Zerubbabel.

In another vision, Zech. 6.1-8, the prophet watches four chariots come out from between two mountains, setting off in the four directions to patrol the earth. The chariot with the black horses goes toward the north country, and the other three, with red, white, and dappled grey horses, go in other directions. The vision ends when the angel, who acts as Zechariah's guide, cries, 'Behold, those who go toward the north country have set my Spirit at rest in the north country' (הניחו את־רוחי בארץ צפון).

Two interpretations of the guide's cryptic statement are possible. The first interprets *ruach* to mean God's anger, and, in a usage attested in Ezek. 5.13, 16.42, 24.13, and 21.22 (although never with *ruach),* gives to הניחו the meaning of 'assuage'. Yahweh's anger is satisfied by giving full vent to it. Thus v. 8 would mean that Yahweh had brought his judgment on Babylon. There is no sure evidence for or against this interpretation although in the first vision (1.7-17) where the horses also appear, they have no function other than patrolling. The LXX translation, τòν θυμόν for *ruchi,* also favors this interpretation.

The second interpretation[42] understands the verse to mean an outpouring of the spirit on the exiles in Babylon, (and also the diaspora scattered in other directions), encouraging them to return to the homeland. The function of the spirit would be similar to that in 4.6, for the purpose of encouraging the return of the exiles is to include them in the temple reconstruction project. In this interpretation הניחו would have the same meaning it had in Number 11 and Isa. 11.2, 'rest upon'. Here it does not rest upon Babylon but upon the exiles in Babylon. The power of the spirit is enlisted in the work of reconstruction. Two things speak in favor of this interpretation. The judgment on Babylon has already been proclaimed in the second vision (2.1-4; RSV 1.18-21). It would be strange if the last vision were to repeat this theme. In addition, the possible return of the exiles to help in the work is mentioned in 6.15, which is then understood to be the prophet's interpretation of the final vision.

---

[42] For the second interpretation cf. F. Horst, *Nahum bis Maleachi* (Tübingen: J.C.B. Mohr, 1954), p. 237; Elliger, *Das Buch der zwölf kleinen Propheten,* p. 106.

Zechariah 6.9-10, which speaks of just such a return, would also be understood as an explanation of this vision. This latter interpretation of an ambiguous passage seems preferable.

F. God's Anger

Finally, in two texts from the exilic period, Job 4.9 and Isa. 27.8, *ruach* is used to mean Yahweh's blasting anger, a meaning which has persisted from the time of the earliest texts.

In his first speech, Eliphaz expresses the opinion that the righteous live long but the wicked die young (Job 4.8-9):

> As I have seen, those who plow iniquity
>   and sow trouble reap the same.
> By the breath of God (מנשמת אלוה) they perish,
>   and by the blast of his anger (מרוח אפו) they are consumed.

That is to say, they are destroyed by God's wrath. The similarity to 2 Sam. 22.16 is readily apparent.[43] In both passages *neshamah, ruach,* and *'aph* appear, although here the *neshamah* stands in a parallelism with *ruach*. The presence of *neshamah* shows that 'breath' rather than 'wind' is meant. But it is possible that there is pictured here an action of *ruach* somewhat different from that in 2 Sam. 22.16 or Exod. 15.8, 10. In those early texts it was the sheer blasting force of the *ruach* on the waters that was described. But here in Job 4.9, it may be the *heat* of the wind, its scorching power, that is suggested more than just its power. In this case אפו must be translated as 'anger', and יכלו 'consumed'. *Ruach* in this case would mean 'power' rather than breath, but it still carries the connotation of anger. Terrien suggests the motif of judgment by cosmic fire.[44] This interpretation aptly continues the agricultural metaphor of v. 8. For those who plow, sow, and reap, it is not the force of the wind so much as the heat of the wind that they fear. The scorching east wind can parch and burn their grain.

The second text using *ruach* with the meaning of anger is Isa. 27.8. It recalls Hos. 13.15 in its use of the east wind to describe the chastising power of Yahweh's *ruach* which Israel experienced in the exile. The verse reads: 'Measure by measure, by exile thou didst con-

---

[43] Friedrich Horst, *Hiob* (BK, Neukirchen: Neukirchener Verlag, 1960), pp. 69-70, has observed the relation of this verse to 2 Sam. 22.16 and Exod. 15.7-19.

[44] Terrien, *Job,* p. 70.

tend with them; he removed them with his fierce blast in the day of
the east wind (הגה ברוחו הקשה ביום קדים)'.

הגה means 'to remove' and is used in only one other text in the
Old Testament, Prov. 25.4-5. There it means both to remove dross
from silver and to remove the wicked from before the king. קשה
means 'hard, severe', as in a hard battle (2 Sam. 2.17), severe servi-
tude (Exod. 1.14), or relentless sword (Isa. 27.1). Because the present text gives good meaning it seems unnecessary to accept Kittel's
suggested emendation of קשה to בקש.

The main problem is the translation of *ruach*. The RSV correctly
suggests the idea of Yahweh's angry power when it translates *ruach*
by 'blast'. Unless the text is emended, there is nothing in the verb
הגה or in the adjective הקשה to suggest a wind. On the contrary,
because the prophet has felt it necessary to add ביום קדים to describe the action of Yahweh's *ruach,* it seems quite evident that he is
not using *ruach* to mean wind, for only if *ruach* means Yahweh's spirit
or his anger would it be necessary to use an additional word meaning wind to describe it metaphorically as wind. No one would say 'a
wind like a wind', but one could say 'anger like the wind.'[45]

It seems evident that *ruach* does not mean wind but rather Yahweh's spirit, with nuances of power and anger. Power is indicated in
the text by the word קשה, illustrated by its use in 27.1. Yahweh's anger is indicated by the fact that the Lord removed Israel and sent
her away like a divorced wife, and also by the prophet's statement
that he 'contended' with Israel. Yahweh sent Israel into exile, punishing her in his anger, and the force of this blow struck Israel like a
blast from the scorching east wind. *Ruach* is used to express both
the anger of Yahweh and his power. But it is his spirit. This interpretation serves to substantiate the interpretation given above for a
similar text, Hos. 13.15.

II. Where is the Spirit to Be Found?:
The Spirit and the Traditions

Having investigated spirit texts related to most of the major Old
Testament traditions, it is now possible to ask the question regard-

---

[45] See Ezek. 13.13, where Yahweh's punishing wrath is compared to a stormy
wind.

ing the Old Testament *Sitz im Leben* of the spirit concept. In which of the traditions was the spirit of God most at home? Under the influence of which school did the concept of God's spirit develop as one of the major themes in the Old Testament?

The three earliest historical traditions, the Yahwist, the Elohist, and the Deuteronomist, need not receive serious consideration. The spirit receives only passing mention in the first two, no mention in the third, and in no case does it appear in texts which directly reflect the style or theology of these major traditions.

Four traditions which linger as possibilities are the royal, priestly, wisdom, and the prophetic.

A. The Royal

With the clear and relatively frequent mention of the spirit in relation to Saul and David it has been assumed by many that the spirit is permanently related to the line of Davidic kings. Furthermore, it has been taken for granted by some scholars that the charismatic gift of the spirit was passed on from father to son in the anointing (coronation) ceremony.[46] This assumption has been made on the basis of 1 Sam. 16.13, in which text the spirit comes on David subsequent to his anointing; and more indirectly, on the basis of Isa. 61.1, which text also relates the gift of the spirit to anointing (of a prophet). It must be observed, however, that never in the Old Testament is the spirit associated with a reigning Davidic king subsequent to David, neither in the historical books, nor in the prophetic books, nor is it even found in the royal psalms where it would be most expected. The spirit departed from the monarchy from the time of Solomon and moved to the prophetic movement. This is entirely in keeping with the nature of the spirit which is spontaneous, free, and charismatic, characteristics which would make the spirit highly out of place in a monarchical institution bound by hereditary succession.

True enough, the spirit is to rest on the future messianic king (Isa. 11.2). But the fact that the prophet must make specific mention of the gift of the spirit, and the fact that he is speaking about a

---

[46] Cf. B.D. Eerdmans, *The Hebrew Book of Psalms* (Leiden: E.J. Brill, 1947), p. 275; H. Weinel, 'רוח und seine Derivate', *ZAW* 18 (1898), pp. 55-56; C.R. North, 'The Religious Aspects of Hebrew Kingship', *ZAW* 50 (1932), pp. 16-17; and Dalglish, *Psalm Fifty-One,* p. 159.

future ideal ruler only underlines the fact that the charismatic gift of the spirit was not assumed to be the permanent possession of all Davidides. Furthermore, Isa. 11.2 is more prophetic than royal.

It can be concluded that the spirit concept, and particularly the charismatic function of the spirit, did not rise out of the royal tradition. The charismatic spirit which could be thought to be most characteristic of the royal office is not associated with the Davidic heirs. Furthermore; it is used as divine designation for non-royal leaders before the monarchy and for others beside monarchs during the period of the monarchy. One must look elsewhere for the locus of the spirit concept.

B. Priestly (Cultic, Legal)

With the exception of Gen. 1.2, where the use of the spirit should be traced to another tradition, (see 'wisdom' below), the Priestly source allows the spirit of God only peripheral activity, so to speak, in that tradition. Neither the laws nor the priesthood, both of which stand at the center of the priestly writing, are in any way related to the spirit of God, a fact which is true also throughout the whole of the Old Testament. The 'priestly-cultic world allowed no room for activity deriving from inspiration'.[47]

Von Rad has pointed out the fact that the charisma, the gift-giving function of the spirit (which aside from Gen. 1.2 is the only way that P uses the spirit), sits loose to the general picture that P has of Israel.[48] Whether this means that the priestly writer has willfully restricted the activity of the spirit of God to peripheral areas such as craftsmanship or leadership ability, or whether he is working with traditions which are foreign to his system, is difficult to determine with any certainty. Because the activity of the spirit is recognized as being present in Joshua,[49] perhaps the latter alternative is the more probable (cf. also Exod. 31.1-3, 'The *Lord* said to Moses … I have filled him with the Spirit of *God*). At any rate, the spirit concept does not appear to be intrinsic to his theological system

---

[47] von Rad, *Theology*, I, p. 99.

[48] von Rad, *Theology*, I, p. 99.

[49] Meaning that the Priestly writer has accepted into his system the tradition implied in Num. 11.28 that Joshua received the spirit as one of the elders. This tradition, however, does not seem to be intrinsic to the Priestly writing because nowhere else in the Priestly source is the spirit recognized as being present charismatically on any of the leaders.

and so can not be said to have derived from, or to have found its home in, the priestly tradition.

C. Wisdom

Job is the only wisdom *book* in the canonical Old Testament which mentions the spirit of God.[50] There are, however, many spirit texts which either in themselves or in their contexts show wisdom influence. These texts can be divided into two categories. There are those that use the spirit of God in relation to creation, either on a cosmic scale or in relation to the creation of human life (but not including those purely prophetic texts which speak of moral recreation). The second category of these wisdom texts speaks of the spirit as the source of wisdom.

The first group of texts, which show wisdom influence and speak of creation, includes Gen. 1.2; Job 26.13; 33.4; 34.14; and Ps. 104.30.[51] With the exception of Ps. 147.18, this list includes all the Old Testament texts which speak of the creator spirit. Or to state it conversely, only Ps. 147.18, among all the Old Testament texts which join spirit to creation, does not give evidence of wisdom influence. One is strongly tempted to propose that this facet of the spirit concept, *spiritus creator*, is rooted in the wisdom tradition. Such a conclusion, however, is threatened by the fact that the Old Testament wisdom literature rarely mentions the spirit of God. Neither Proverbs nor Ecclesiastes uses it. Furthermore none of the classical wisdom texts mention it, neither Proverbs 8 nor Job 28, nor is it mentioned in the wisdom psalms. It is a question whether the wisdom school ever worked with the concept of the spirit of God.

It is preferable to think of the cosmic creator spirit concept as being rooted in an independent creation tradition originally joined to neither the priestly nor the wisdom traditions. It appears to exist in embryonic form in Gen. 2.7. To the extent that wisdom used this creation tradition it also took over the *spiritus creator* concept.

---

[50] *Ruach* in Prov. 1.23 is considered by some to be the spirit of God (cf. Lys, *Ruach, le Souffle dans l'Ancien Testament*, p. 302), but should rather be thought of, analogous to Job 32.18, as the human spirit. The 'human' is Wisdom personified as a woman; cf. P. van Imschoot, 'Sagesse et Esprit dans l'AT', *Revue Biblique* 47 (1938), pp. 27, 34.

[51] For the wisdom strain in Genesis 1, cf. von Rad, *Theology*, I, p. 143. For wisdom influence in Psalm 33, cf. McKane, *Prophets and Wise Men*, p. 85. The wisdom context of the other texts is obvious.

The second group of texts, in which the spirit of God is described as the source of wisdom (Gen. 41.38 (E); Isa. 11.2; Job 32.8; Exod. 28.3; 31.3; 35.31; Deut. 34.9; [Num. 27.18]; Dan. 4.5, 6, 15; 5.11, 14) is even less firmly joined to the wisdom tradition. Most of these texts are related in some way to the prophetic tradition.[52]

Even in the case of the spirit on Joshua in the Priestly source, it is possible that there is present the influence of the prophetic school on the priestly writings (cf. Num. 27.18; Deut. 34.9 as related to Num. 11.25, 28), while the rather peculiar conjunction of 'Lord' and 'God' in the Bezalel narrative of Exod. 31.1-3 (the *Lord* speaks of the spirit of *God*) probably indicated that the priestly school was working with an old tradition which may have undergone prophetic influence in another day.

It is evident that only under prophetic influence has the spirit of God concept penetrated the wisdom tradition (except in the case of the creation texts). Old wisdom traced the source of human wisdom to experience or to education, with no reference to a divine source. Under the influence of the prophetic tradition the wisdom school acknowledged that God through his spirit was the source, perhaps the only source, of true wisdom. In other words, it is the prophetic tradition which has declared the spirit of God to be the source of true wisdom.[53]

D. Prophetic

The relationship between the prophetic movement and the spirit texts in the pre-exilic period was noted above. This relationship is by no means reversed in the exilic period. Even subtracting the texts related even tenuously to wisdom, one is still left with the large majority of texts which are from prophetic oracles. If one were to add the texts above which, even though showing wisdom elements, are still basically prophetic in their use of the spirit, one is impressed by the overall relation of the spirit and prophecy. Except, perhaps, for those *spiritus creator* texts which very possibly belonged originally to an independent creation tradition, it can be concluded

---

[52] Genesis 41.38 is in the Elohist source. Prophetic characteristics in Job 32 have been noted by Imschoot, 'Sagesse et Esprit', p. 34, and Terrien, *Job* (IB), p. 1131. For the Daniel texts see below, Chapter 6. Norman Porteous, *Daniel* (Philadelphia, Westminster, 1965), pp. 14-17, has emphasized the elements in Daniel which stand in the old prophetic tradition.

[53] A fact noted by Imschoot, 'Sagesse et Esprit', p. 46.

that the spirit of God concept sprang from and was used by the prophetic tradition.

III. The Spirit and Early Judaism

With the fall of Babylon to Cyrus in 538 BCE came the formation of the Persian empire and the first return of the exiles to Jerusalem (Ezra 1). How extensive this return under Sheshbazzar was and what concrete changes it brought in Judah are not known. The return under Zerubbabel sometime before 520 BCE is more thoroughly documented. Ezra 2-6, Haggai, and Zechariah 1-8 give information not only about the return but also concerning the rebuilding of the temple, completed in 516 BCE. Information about this religious community formed about the second temple, sometimes referred to as early Judaism, is admittedly scant. Parts of Isaiah 55-66, Joel, Obadiah, and Malachi can be gleaned for information about this period, extending to 460 BCE. This was the early restoration of the covenant community, organized under the leadership of the high priest as a part of one of the western provinces of the Persian empire. It is a restoration which is to be redone more thoroughly under Ezra and Nehemiah in the middle of the fifth century BCE.

Certain groups of texts from this period represent the beginnings of Judaism more than the development of the classic theology inherited from the major pre-exilic prophets. In their common interest in and emphasis on the cult, the sacerdotal system, and the law, their description of the activity of the spirit is cast in a mold which differs radically, both from the wisdom literature mentioned above, and more particularly, from the prophets, Deutero-Isaiah, Ezekiel, and Joel. The literature of this period which falls in this category includes the Priestly source, Haggai, Zechariah, Trito-Isaiah, and Ezekiel 40-48. In the Priestly source, the spirit is placed in the service of the cult in the manufacturing of the temple furniture or the priestly garments. Even the spirit on Joshua does not place him at the head of Israel's armies as in the days of the judges, but authenticates him as the successor of Moses, the lawgiver. In Haggai and Zechariah the power and encouragement of the spirit is enlisted in the work of temple reconstruction. Trito-Isaiah, in a text which should be classified as early Judaism (59.21),[54] emphasizes the status quo, with the assurance that the old covenant remains valid through the continuing presence of the spirit. Ezekiel 40-48 has the distinction of being the only juridical body of literature that mentions the spirit of God (43.5) but in a way completely unrelated to the main theme of those chapters, the reconstituted Jewish theocracy in Jerusalem. In this literature of early Judaism the impression is left that the spirit can be dispensed with altogether, that it is not a constitutive factor in the system. Where the spirit is mentioned, it is used to underwrite projects which have started without the spirit, and can proceed very well without it. There is missing the interiority, the moral vitality, the driving purposiveness, the impending manifestation in power, which characterizes the spirit. This trend towards externalization will become even more evident in the later and final period of the Old Testament.

---

[54] As is commonly recognized, Isaiah 56-66 contains a variety of material. Neither 61.1-11 nor 63.7-19 falls into the category of literature from early Judaism, but rather in their early exilic dating and close similarity to Deutero-Isaiah should be classed with Deutero-Isaiah, Ezekiel 1-39, and Joel. However, in regard to Isa. 59.21, its similarity to Deut. 3.14, and to the phraseology of the Priestly source, places it definitely together with literature from early Judaism.

6

'THE SPIRIT CAME UPON JAHAZIEL': FROM EZRA TO DANIEL

I. The Spirit under the Law

With the return to Jerusalem of Ezra in 458 BCE (Ezra 7) and of Nehemiah in 444 BCE (Nehemiah 2), the stage was set for the reconstruction of the covenant community around the law. This was not only approved, it was authorized by the Persian authorities for the purpose of creating a strong buffer province on the west end of the Persian empire facing Egypt.

Under Nehemiah as governor, Jerusalem's walls were rebuilt and the administration of the Jewish province was reorganized. But the major part of the religious reformation was carried out under the direction of Ezra, the 'scribe skilled in the law of Moses'. This reorganization around the written law (possibly the Pentateuch) was necessary to ensure the survival of the Jewish community against interior disintegration or the inroads of the pagan world.

> Israel's transition from nation to a law community had been made. As such she would thenceforth exist, and this she could do without statehood and even though scattered all over the world. The distinguishing mark of a Jew would not be political nationality, nor primarily ethnic background, nor even regular participation in the Temple cult (impossible for Jews of the Diaspora), but adherence to the law of Moses.[1]

This adherence to the law is the characteristic of this period which most influenced the employment of the spirit of God concept. For the fact is that the spirit of God is rarely mentioned in the

---

[1] John Bright, *A History of Israel* (Philadelphia; Westminster, 1959), p. 375.

literature of this period.[2] This is because, in a community organized around the law, there is no longer the anticipation of the direct inspiration of the spirit, the unmediated guidance offered by Yahweh's *ruach*. The activity of the spirit is free and uncoerced, setting it in opposition to religious life organized on the basis of law.

Concomitant with the disappearance of the spirit is the cessation of any prophetic activity, a result which could be anticipated in a community organized under the law. The priest and the scribe, those who are skilled in interpreting the law, replace the prophet who claims to speak directly for God. Because heretofore the spirit has been inseparably and almost exclusively joined to the prophetic movement one can expect the mention of the spirit of God to disappear along with the disappearance of prophetic literature. In the literature of this period there is no recognition of the present activity of the spirit in anything like the profound manner in which it was described in Isaiah or Ezekiel, in Job or Joel. There is no glance into the future, no expectation of an approaching outpouring of God's power through his spirit, no consciousness of the renewing and regenerating activity of the spirit. There is only a bare memory of such a spirit in Nehemiah, and in Chronicles, a conscious imitation of older categories cast in a contemporary mode. Only in Daniel, representing the apocalyptic literature which succeeded the prophetic and was increasingly popular from the second century BCE, is there to be seen in a contemporary setting the persistence of a genuine pre-exilic category of the spirit. The description given for the spirit in early Judaism as being only a peripheral influence in that period can also be applied to the present period. The spirit of God plays no vital part in events of this period and, as such, remains little more than a memory of past glories.

II. Levitical 'Prophets'

In the reconstructed Jewish community from which the book of Chronicles derived, some from among the Levites were considered the heirs of the prophets, and as such were considered also to have inherited the gift of the spirit. But the spirit of God inspired in

---

[2] Texts from this period, 460 to 165 BCE, are: 1 Chron. 12.19; 2 Chron. 15.1; 18.23; 20.14; 24.20; Neh. 9.20, 30; Ps. 147.18 (dated to this period because of vv. 2 and 13 which point to the time of Nehemiah); and Dan. 4.5, 6, 15; 5.11, 14.

them primarily the gift of eloquence or the poetic gift, their manner of speaking, rather than, as was the case for the classical prophets, the actual content of their message.[3]

1 Chronicles 12.17-19 (RSV 16-18) pictures the scene as some of the fighting men from Judah and Benjamin came to David at Ziklag to join forces with him. David meets them with a short greeting, questioning them about their motives in joining him. The answer is given by Amasai, the spokesman of the group, (v. 19; RSV 18):

> Then the Spirit came upon Amasai (ורוח לבשה את־עמשי)
> chief of the thirty, and he said,
>> 'We are yours, O David;
>>> and with you, O son of Jesse!
>> Peace, peace to you,
>>> and peace to your helpers!
>> For your God helps you.'

The verb לבשה ('clothed'), translated here as 'came upon', is that used of the spirit on Gideon (Judg. 6.34), probably because Amasai also is a warrior. But instead of stirring him up to feats of military valor, it moves him to eloquence. The spirit inspires the rhetorical gift.

2 Chronicles 15.1 describes a scene in which Asa, king of Judah, upon returning from a successful encounter with Zerah, the king of Egypt, is greeted by a short speech urging him to institute a religious reform:

> The spirit of God came upon Azariah (היתה עליו רוח אלהים)
> the son of Oded, and he went out to meet Asa, and said to him,
> 'Hear me, Asa, and all Judah and Benjamin: The Lord is with
> you, while you are with him ... But you, take courage! Do not let
> your hands be weak, for your work shall be rewarded'. When Asa

---

[3] Cf. Eichrodt, *Theology*, I, p. 337, who writes, 'whereas in pre-exilic times the temple police looked after the disciplining of recalcitrant ecstatics (Jer. 20.16; 29.26), later generations would not tolerate even the form of preaching in independence of the Law and attempted in various ways to create a substitute. Poetic inspiration and musical gifts are now characterized as the operation of *ruach,* and in particular the temple prophets' ability to improvise liturgical utterances is prized as demonstrating his prophetic status (Ps. 49.4; 1 Chron. 15.22, 27; 25.1-3; 2 Chron. 20.14). At this point the prophet is finally absorbed into the ranks of the temples officials.'

heard these words, the prophecy of Azariah, the son of Oded (MT the prophecy, Oded the prophet), he took courage, and put away the abominable idols … (2 Chron. 15.1-8).

The speech had its effect and Asa put away the idols, repaired the altar, renewed the covenant, and removed the idolatrous queen mother, Maacah.

As in the preceding passage, the spirit inspires eloquence. Galling has pointed out that the situation in which the speech is laid is artificial, and that the exhortation should be considered, as von Rad has shown, an example of a style of preaching current in Levitical circles in the Chronicler's own time.[4] If this is true, it means that the description of the work of the spirit given here reflects the attitude towards the spirit of God during the Chronicler's time, rather than during the tenth century. The Levites considered themselves the heirs of the prophets in that they were the ones who were inspired by the spirit.[5] But their prophecy was not an oracle but an oration.[6] It must be concluded, then, that in this passage the spirit is credited with having inspired a prophet and a prophecy of a former day, but in reality it reflects rather the view that the spirit inspired those who preached like the Levitical priests of 400 BCE.

2 Chronicles 20.14-15 describes a scene before an impending battle between Judah, led by King Jehoshaphat, and the invading Moabite and Ammonite armies. After a prayer led by the king in the presence of the assembly of Judah, gathered in the house of the Lord,

the Spirit of the Lord came (היתה עליו רוח יהוה) upon Jahaziel the son of Zechariah, son of Benaiah, son of Mattaniah, a Levite of the sons of Asaph … And he said, 'Hearken, all Judah

---

[4] Kurt Galling, *Die Bücher der Chronik* (ATD; Göttingen: Vandenhoeck und Ruprecht, 1954), p. 114. Galling refers to the comments of G. von Rad, 'Die levitische Predigt in den Büchern der Chronik', in Albrecht Alt (ed.), *Festschrift Otto Procksch zum sechzigsten Geburtstag* (Leipzig: Deichert, 1934), p. 117, also found in von Rad, *Gesammelte Studien*, I, p. 248.

[5] Cf. von Rad, *Theology*, I, p. 101.

[6] Cf. Lys, *Ruach, le Souffle dans l'Ancien Testament*, p. 185. Adam C. Welch, *The Work of the Chronicler* (London: Oxford Press, 1939), pp. 49-50, has noted the stereotyped nature of these prophetic speeches in Chronicles as well as their difference in comparison with the oracles of the classical prophets.

... Thus says the Lord to you, 'Fear not, and be not dismayed at this great multitude; for the battle is not yours but God's ...'

The verb, the same as in 15.1, was found in Judg. 3.10 and 11.29 (and elsewhere in the earliest period). The situation is different from 15.1, for here Jahaziel encourages Judah to fight courageously, it being Yahweh's battle. But the function of the spirit does not vary. It inspires the speech which, this time, is delivered by 'a Levite of the sons of Asaph', substantiating what was suggested above. The spirit inspires the eloquence of Jahaziel, one of those Levites who were perhaps the cult prophets[7] of early Judaism.

It may be significant that a king (2 Chron. 32.7-8) can give the same kind of speech with no mention of its inspiration by the spirit of God. It is possible that the spirit as the inspirer of rhetoric was thought to be the exclusive possession[8] of the temple prophets, who represented one rank in the class of Levitical priests (cf. 1 Chron. 25.1-3, where it is stated repeatedly that the Levites 'prophesied'). At any rate, the king, in spite of his rhetoric, and probably because he is the king, is denied the inspiration of the spirit of God claimed by the Levites.

In Chronicles there is the persistence of the charismatic spirit, the heir, so to speak, of the prophetic spirit. It is interesting to note that the function of the spirit in these three verses is similar to that in 2 Sam. 23.2, a text from the earliest period. There too the spirit inspired the poetic and rhetorical gift in the 'sweet psalmist of Israel'.

III. Daniel the Seer

Five times in the book of Daniel it is said of Daniel that 'the spirit of the holy gods' (רוח אלהין קדישין) was in him. The phrase is used

---

[7] Cf. W.A.L. Elmslie, *Chronicles*, in IB, III, p. 426, and Aubrey R. Johnson, *The Cultic Prophet in Ancient Israel* (Cardiff: University of Wales Press, 1962), p. 75.

[8] But perhaps 'exclusive' is too strong a word because the spirit has also been attributed to Amasai, the *warrior*. It can hardly be argued that the presence of the spirit in 1 Chron. 12.19 is genuine historical recollection, for this verse shows all the characteristics of being the Chronicler's framework; cf. also the same editorial framework in 2 Chron. 15.1, 20.14, 24.20, and compare with 2 Chron. 18.23, a narrative transferred verbatim from an earlier source where there is no such framework. Perhaps because of his rhetorical skill, Amasai was considered an anonymous Levite!

in 4.5, 6, and 15 by Nebuchadnezzar as he relates his dream and calls for Daniel to give its interpretation. Verse 18 says significantly, 'This dream I, King Nebuchadnezzar, saw. And you, O Belteshazzar, declare the interpretation, because all the wise men of my kingdom are not able to make known to me the interpretation, but you are able, for the spirit of the holy gods is in you'. It is used again by Belshazzar and his queen in 5.11, 14, and again in connection with the interpretation of the mysterious writing on the wall which appeared during Belshazzar's feast. In 5.14, Belshazzar addresses Daniel: 'I have heard of you that the spirit of the holy gods is in you, and that light and understanding and excellent wisdom are found in you'. Because the wise men of Babylon have not been able to read the writing, the king asks Daniel to interpret it.

There are amazing parallels with the Joseph narrative in Genesis 41. Neither the wise men and magicians of Babylon nor of Egypt are able to interpret the dream (Gen. 41.8; Dan. 4.4; 5.15). An Israelite is called in who can interpret the dream because God will give him the interpretation (Gen. 41.16; Dan. 4.5, 6, 15; 5.11, 14). He is to be promoted to a high governmental position (Gen. 41.41; Dan. 5.16), and receives a non-Jewish name (Gen. 41.45; Dan. 4.5) The similarity extends even to the terminology used. Not only רוח and אלהים in its Aramaic equivalent, but the word פעם, meaning to be troubled, used only five times in the Old Testament, is used in Gen. 41.8 and in Dan. 2.1, 3 (also Judg. 13.25; Ps. 77.5) in the introductory section of the dream sequence. Finally, the wisdom influence is seen in both passages (cf. Gen. 41.39, Dan. 5.11, 14).

The similarities between the Joseph and Daniel texts lead to the conclusion, first of all, that the translation of אלהין as in Gen. 41.38, should be 'God' rather than 'gods'. This translation is further confirmed by Dan. 2.18 and 2.28, in which Daniel indicates that it is only his own God who can make known dreams and their interpretation.[9] Significant differences however appear in the actual interpretation of the function of the spirit in the two texts. Granted, in both cases it is the charismatic spirit given to exceptional men of God. But in the earlier text Joseph is given the ability of leadership,

---

[9] Cf. J.A. Montgomery, *The Book of Daniel* (NY: Charles Scribner's Sons, 1927), p. 225, and Koch, *Geist und Messias,* p. 33, n. 12. Arthur Jeffery, *The Book of Daniel,* in IB, VI, p. 409, says that 4.34 shows that the king is using the divine name with a singular meaning.

rhetoric, wise counsel. In the latter text, however, it is the ability to interpret dreams which is granted to Daniel through the spirit of God, a talent in Joseph which is in no way related to the spirit (cf. 41.15-16).

This description, joined with the spirit in the Joseph narrative, of the well-cultivated young man skilled in rhetoric, leadership, and counsel has been described as one of the characteristics of the so-called 'old wisdom'. This old wisdom which Israel shared with her neighbors, especially Egypt, is found even in the earliest Old Testament literature and is particularly characteristic of the pre-exilic period.[10] The later description of the sage as a seer with knowledge of the secrets of the future only became possible after the fusion of wisdom with apocalyptic at the very end of the Old Testament period.[11] Therefore, regardless of the remarkable similarity of the Joseph and Daniel texts, and in spite of the fact that they share the charisma-granting spirit of God concept, in view of the actual content of the charisma one is justified in dating these two texts at opposite poles of the Old Testament period.

The spirit of God in Daniel is the charismatic spirit which grants special talents and abilities, and in this case, the ability to interpret dreams (wiser than the wise men of Babylon) and predict the future.

IV. 'He makes his wind blow'

Psalm 147.18, a creation hymn, describes Yahweh's spirit under the metaphor of a wind: 'He sends forth his word, and melts them (ice); he makes his wind blow (רוחו ישב) and the waters flow'.

Just as the texts from Chronicles describe the coming of the spirit with verbs used elsewhere of the spirit only in the earliest period (cf. 1 Chron. 12.19 with Judg. 6.34, or 2 Chron. 15.1 with Judg. 3.10); and just as the Daniel texts show remarkable similarity in form and content to Gen. 41.38 from the earliest period; so also the psalm text dated to this period, 147.18, 'he makes his wind blow', uses terminology which is used elsewhere in the Old Testament only in Exod. 15.10, 'thou didst blow with thy wind'. These similari-

---

[10] von Rad, *Theology,* I, pp. 429-40.
[11] von Rad, *Theology,* I, p. 451.

ties represent conscious archaisms and are illustrative of the fact that this late period is using the spirit of God not as a living concept but as a memory of the past.

The translation of 'wind' is possible but 'breath' is preferable. In a context of creation (v. 4) and of the providential care of God for his creation (vv. 8-9, 16-18), the wind is nowhere else in the Old Testament assigned the role given to *ruach* in v. 18. Furthermore the parallelism with 'word' suggests Yahweh's breath rather than the natural wind (cf. Ps. 33.6; Gen. 1.2-3; 2 Sam. 22.16). The verse is similar to Job 37.10, whose use of *neshamah* (breath) excludes the translation of 'wind'.

By the use of the ambiguous *ruach* in Ps. 147.18 the psalmist meant to suggest the action of the warm wind which melts ice, together with the action of Yahweh's breath which articulates the word, both included in the life-bestowing activity of the spirit of God which sustains and preserves the life of the natural world. This is the only text in this final period which speaks of the creative spirit of God.

V. The Good Old Days

Several texts from this period recall the activity of the spirit in an earlier day. Because 2 Chron. 18.23 is a duplicate of 1 Kgs. 22.24, it has no direct connection with a post-exilic situation.

2 Chronicles 24.20-21, contained in a narrative not duplicated in the book of Kings, shows evidence of the Chronicler's editorializing and may reflect a post-exilic spirit concept. The verse describes the action of Zechariah, the son of the high priest, in rebuking King Joash for his unfaithfulness.

> Then the Spirit of God took possession of (לבשה ורוח אלהים) Zechariah the son of Jehoida the priest; and he stood above the people, and said to them, 'Thus says God, 'Why do you transgress the commandments of the Lord, so that you cannot prosper? Because you have forsaken the Lord, he has forsaken you'. But they conspired against him, and by command of the king they stoned him ...

In contrast to the Levitical speeches described above, this chapter describes what appears to be a true prophetic oracle. It is woe rather than weal, denunciation rather than praise, plain-spoken rather than florid. In a singular way it lacks the rhetorical flourish characteristic of the Levitical speeches; instead it contains the sort of prophetic rebuke heard frequently during the period of the great prophets. In this case, the spirit of God appears in a role familiar to another day, inspiring the prophetic word, the contents of the message, rather than the manner of presentation.

Because of the presence of the Chronicler's editorial framework (v. 20a), it seems clear that the editor recognized and spoke approvingly of the action of the prophetic spirit of God in a past day.

In this respect, the above text resembles Neh. 9.20 and 9.30 which also view the spirit in retrospect. Contained in a prayer of Ezra (according to the LXX) and following a reference to the golden calf and the pillar of cloud and fire, 9.20 reads: 'Thou gavest thy good Spirit to instruct them (ורוחך הטובה נתתי להשכילם) and didst not withhold thy manna from their mouth, and gavest them water for their thirst'. Expressed in terms popularly used in the wisdom school (שכל, טוב),[12] the verse, joined as it is to the gift of manna and following the preceding historical sequence, apparently refers to the gift of the spirit on Moses and the elders (Num. 11.17, 25).[13] In this case it was considered, in retrospect, to be a guide, leading and instructing the people through the elders.[14] Although it is not expressly stated, the instruction was probably in the law (vv. 13-14), which by this time in the scribal circles had been joined to the wisdom teaching[15] (cf. for example, Psalms 1; 19; 119). If this verse can be said to contain a wisdom element, it would be the only place in

---

[12] Thierry Maertens, *Le Souffle et l'Esprit de Dieu* (Bruges: Desclee De Brouwer, 1959), p. 50, believes that הטובה also represents a wisdom element in the spirit, the spirit as educative, rearing and guiding with prudence.

[13] Thus Galling, *Chronik*, p. 237.

[14] It is possible to translate השכילם by 'to prosper them' (cf. BDB, p. 968). If it is to be taken in conjunction with the food, drink, and clothing which immediately follow in the context, this might be the best translation. However, in the historical narratives the giving of the manna or water is never related to the giving of the spirit in any way. For this reason, and following the meaning given in Ps. 143.10, it seems preferable to translate it as 'instruct'.

[15] Cf. J. Lindblom, 'Wisdom in the Old Testament Prophets', in M. Noth and D. Winton Thomas (eds.), *Wisdom in Israel and in The Ancient Near East* (Leiden: E.J. Brill, 1955), p. 196.

the Old Testament where wisdom and the law are joined with the spirit.[16]

The reference of this verse is to the distant past but the description of the spirit as a 'good' spirit, teaching and instructing Israel in the way of the law, reflects a conception of the spirit current in Ezra's time. Just as the Priestly source placed the spirit in the service of the cult, so here the author has placed the spirit in the service of the law. The concept of the spirit which appears here stands in definite contrast to the prophetic spirit of another day. Nehemiah 9.30, similar in many ways to Zech. 7.12, ascribes the prophetic warning of a past era to the inspiration of the spirit: 'many years thou didst bear with them, and didst warn them by thy Spirit through thy prophets (ברוחך ביד־נביאיך)'. Here also, as in 2 Chron. 24.20, the primary activity of the spirit in former times was recognized as being the inspiration of the prophetic word.

VI. Conclusion

The end of the prophetic movement coincided with, or perhaps was encouraged by, the advent of the community of the law. The teacher of the law replaced the proclaimer of God's word as the leader in the reconstructed community. The law, by nature, precluded the activity of the spirit. Until this period, the spirit of God has been associated closely with the covenants, both old and new. But now that the covenant has been replaced by the law (or reinterpreted in terms of the law) as the constituting factor in the reconstructed Jewish community, the spirit's base of operation has been taken away. It can no longer be the spirit of power active at the center of the covenant community. Only the advent of the new covenant will again make this possible.

Finally, the fact that wisdom was joined to the law meant that any contact it had previously had with the spirit through the prophetic influence, notably in Job, was cut off. The end result is that the spirit of God no longer is active in the main stream of Judaism, as it is represented in the Old Testament, but is shifted to an ancillary role, found only on the periphery of the religious life of the re-

---

[16] However, the spirit does not inspire the law, but only leads Israel to follow it. McKane, *Prophets and Wise Men,* p. 110, sees a wisdom element here.

constructed community, contributing little more than ornamentation to its religion. The omens observed in the texts of early Judaism, the Priestly source, III Isaiah, Haggai, and Zechariah, turned out to be a true indication of the course that the spirit would take in full-bodied Judaism. It could only move from the periphery to almost total exclusion.

7

'WHEREVER THE SPIRIT WOULD GO THEY WENT': THE SPIRIT'S RELATION TO YAHWEH

I. How to Recognize a Person

Is there any significant personalizing of the spirit in the Old Testament? This is the central problem involved in a discussion of the relation of the spirit to Yahweh. A significant personalization has been seen by some scholars particularly in certain post-exilic texts. Thus Eichrodt, in speaking about the texts of early Judaism, finds a

> development by which the spirit of God is made markedly independent, so that it can now be portrayed as a so-called hypostasis, that is to say, a separate entity which acts of its own motion, and is of itself concerned with human affairs … A man's attitude toward it determines his attitude to God; disobedience to the holy spirit grieves it, and causes it to withdraw, with the result that the flow of divine life is cut off.[1]

He is referring, of course, to the spirit in Isa. 63.10 and Ps. 51.13 (RSV 51.11).

In examining the problem of personalization of the spirit in the Old Testament, certain criteria for judging the presence or absence of this process are available. These criteria can be applied to specific texts and to the period as a whole. It is assumed that if personalization appears in the Old Testament it would be most likely to appear in later rather than earlier texts.

If there is a significant degree of personalization it should be indicated by anyone or more of the following evidences.

---

[1] Cf. Eichrodt, *Theology*, II, p. 60.

1. The spirit appears alone, acting independently of Yahweh. A very clear example of this is found in 1 Kgs 22.19-23 Here the lying spirit, distinguished from the spirit of Yahweh in v. 24, appears before Yahweh, addresses him, and receives his commands.

2. Verbs or adjectives which indicate personalization are used with the spirit. If the spirit were to speak, to weep, to be sad, to move forward, for example, it would appear to be personified.

3. There is a significant increase in the use of the masculine gender for the spirit.[2] *Ruach* is normally considered a feminine gender noun. In some cases, however, it becomes masculine as indicated by a masculine verb or adjective. If this tendency to use the masculine rather than the feminine gender for the spirit should show a marked pattern of increase from early to later texts, it might indicate personalization.

4. If there is evidenced an increase in the use of the article with the spirit, personalization may be evidenced.

5. The use of the personal pronoun would indicate personalization, as it does, for instance, in 1 Kgs 22.21-22. The personal pronoun, however, never appears as a surrogate for the spirit of God in the Old Testament. Never is the spirit referred to as he, she, or it.

II. Does the Spirit Proceed Alone?

It has been suggested that the spirit was one of the concepts through which the 'omnipresence and immanence of God were maintained in spite of the growing belief in his transcendence'.[3] If this were true, both a growing trend towards the personalization of the spirit, together with the gradual withdrawal of Yahweh from intimate association with his people could be expected. That this did not happen, in this post-exilic period at least, is best illustrated by Isa. 63.7-14 where, to be sure, many have wished to discern a pronounced hypostasization of the spirit. But where in the Old Testament could there be found a passage which expresses more clearly the intimate relation between Yahweh himself and his people, and in which precisely just that 'transcendence' is more lacking? To be

---

[2] Cf. E. Kautzsch, *Gesenius' Hebrew Grammar* (Oxford: Clarendon Press, 1910), p. 392, §122o(d).

[3] Schoemaker, 'The Use of רוח in the Old Testament and πνεῦμα in the New Testament', p. 28.

sure, unusual things are attributed to the spirit in this passage, but they are likewise ascribed to Yahweh as well. There is nothing 'distant' about the God described in this text. He could not be closer to his people than he is pictured here.

Similar statements could be made about Psalm 51 or 139. In the former, it was the extremely intimate nature of the relation between the psalmist and Yahweh which was used as an argument against interpreting the 'presence' of v. 13 (RSV v. 11) as a cultic presence. Psalm 139 contains no objective discussion of the 'omni' characteristics of God: his omniscience, omnipresence, and omnipotence. It is instead a meditation on the intimate communion with his Lord experienced by the psalmist. Both of these texts, Psalms 51 and 139, show the closest possible relationship between Yahweh and his creation.

Furthermore, the consideration of other individual post-exilic texts does not give evidence of an independent action of the spirit apart from Yahweh.

For example, the spirit in Ezek. 1.12, although at first glance rather ambiguous in this respect, actually refers to Yahweh's own will, his freedom of decision. This is one of the few texts in the Old Testament in which the spirit stands in an interior relation to Yahweh with no apparent reference to the created world. There can be no thought here of a personalized mediator standing between Yahweh and his creation.

Again, the spirit which enters into Ezekiel and sets him on his feet (2.2) might give evidence of independent action. But the same effect of the spirit's working is predicated of the hand of the Lord (cf. 8.3 and 40.1-2), while the spirit is identified as the spirit of God in 11.24. Just as it is difficult to conceive of the hand of the Lord having separate action, so the action of the spirit must not be considered an independent action but rather the work of Yahweh himself.

In 1 Chron. 12.19 it is 'the spirit' that comes upon Amasai with no word linking the spirit to Yahweh. But in all the other Chronicles texts it is identified as either the spirit of God or the spirit of the Lord.

Isaiah 32.15, 'until the spirit is poured upon us from on high', also has the spirit standing alone, so to speak. But the passive verb, and the phrase 'from on high' both point away from an independent action of the spirit.

Isaiah 34.16, 'his Spirit has gathered them', with its transitive verb, might be evidence for an independent action; but the possessive pronoun relates it quite closely to Yahwe. Furthermore, the fact that the parallel member of the strophe is 'the mouth of the Lord has commanded' seems to exclude the thought of an independently acting spirit.

Actually, in almost all of the post-exilic texts the spirit is qualified either by the divine name or possessive pronoun; or, it is placed in a parallel with the mouth, the hand, the breath of Yahwe as if to preclude interpretation as an independent being, acting on its own initiative. In this respect there is also little change from texts of the earlier, pre-exilic periods.

III. The Spirit's Entourage

A. Verbs

Never is a verb used of the spirit of God which unconditionally qualifies it as a person. In the earliest texts in Judges and 1 Samuel (repeated in the latest period in Chronicles, the verbs 'leaped upon' (Judg. 14.6; 1 Sam. 10.6, 10) and 'clothed' (Judg. 6.34; 1 Chron. 12.19) are used metaphorically to describe the violent effects of the appearance of the spirit. They are not used to designate the nature of the spirit itself. In the case of other unusual words, for example, 'stand' (Hag. 2.5) and 'pour out' (Joel 3.1 RSV 2.28), they are verbs that are also used of inanimate objects. They are, in addition, used in texts that give not the slightest hint of personalization.

B. Adjectives

The only adjectives used to modify spirit are 'holy' (Isa. 63.10; Ps. 51.13 RSV 51.11) and 'good' (Neh. 9.20; Ps. 143.10). These are adjectives which are also applied to inanimate objects and cannot in themselves indicate either personalization or separation from Yahweh.

In Ps. 143.10, however, 'good spirit' has reminded some commentators of the good and bad spirits in the Persian Zoroastrian religion.[4] Perhaps the omission of the article here with the adjective, its use being normally expected according to the rules of Hebrew grammar,[5] was deliberate in order to avoid the suggestion of personalization and confusion with the good spirit in the Persian religion.

C. Gender

In cases where it can be determined, the gender of *ruach* does not warrant a conclusion in favor of personalization. In the latest texts the masculine is never evidenced. In the whole period subsequent to 593 BCE, the masculine is used in only two passages, Isa. 34.16, and Ezek. 1.12 (in the latter text probably to distinguish it from the wind in v. 4 which is feminine). Actually the masculine gender is found most frequently in the late pre-exilic texts, where it would be least expected if it were being used to indicate a personalization or separation of the spirit from Yahweh.

D. The Article

The article is rarely used in any period and never in the texts of the latest period. Also it should be noted that, with the exception of Ezek. 1.12, the article is never used with the masculine gender. If the article is used, the gender is feminine, and when the masculine gender is present the article is missing.

IV. Can the Spirit Grieve?

Because Isa. 63.10 is singled out by commentators as evidence of personalization, separate consideration will be given to this text: 'But they rebelled and grieved his holy spirit'. The fact that the spirit is said to grieve is taken to mean that the spirit is a person.[6]

The verb translated 'grieved' is עצבו. The fact that it is a transitive verb denoting action *upon* the spirit, and not intransitive, describing an emotion of the spirit, is important, for it is usually in-

---

[4] Cf. Kraus, *Psalmen,* p. 938, who notes this Persian background but denies any such reference here.

[5] Cf. Kautzsch, *Gesenius' Hebrew Grammar,* p. 408, §126u, an omission pointed out by Briggs and Briggs, *Psalms,* p. 518.

[6] Cf. Skinner, *Genesis,* p. 222, who attributes to Isa. 63.10 the 'highest degree of personification of the Spirit attained in the Old Testament'; and Delitzsch, *Isaiah,* who describes the Spirit in terms of 'an existence capable of feeling and therefore not a mere force'.

terpreted in the latter sense. The verb in *qal* is עצב. It is true that in the *niphal* this verb can have the sense of 'grieving for something', as David grieved for Absalom (2 Sam. 19.2), or 'feeling' physical pain, as when a stone-cutter is struck by a flying stone (Eccl. 10.9). But neither the *qal,* the *piel,* nor the *hiphil* carries such a meaning in any text in the Old Testament; and the verb in Isa. 63.10 is *piel.* Judging from the use of the word in the Old Testament, the transitive sense of this verb appears to be one of *imposing one's will* on someone or something, or of opposing one's will against another's. For example, 1 Kgs 1.6 says of Adonijah: 'His father had never at anytime *displeased* (עצבו) him by asking, 'Why have you done thus and so?' That is, David had never opposed Adonijah nor crossed his will. In 1 Chron. 4.10 it is written of Jabez that he 'called on the God of Israel, saying, "Oh that thou wouldst bless me and enlarge my border and that thou wouldst keep me from harm so that it might not *hurt* (עצבי) me'''. It was not the physical pain or psychological grief he sought to avoid, but as is clear from the context, he is asking to be protected from any opposition that will hurt his chances of enlarging his estate. Psalm 56.5 expresses it even more clearly: 'All day long they seek to injure (יעצבו) my cause; all their thoughts are against me for evil'. The Psalmist's enemies are opposing him, seeking to frustrate him in all he attempts to do. Even when עצב is used in a purely physical sense, as in Job 10.8 or Jer. 44.19, the fundamental meaning is to shape an object according to the maker's will. This must also apply to the verb and its object in Isa. 63.10. Instead of 'grieved', the translation should be 'opposed' or 'resisted'. The writer did not intend to say that the spirit 'grieved', but he did mean to say that Israel had opposed the spirit of Yahweh when she rebelled against his guidance (v. 10a). *Ruach* means Yahweh's holy will. This not only eliminates the interpretation of *ruach* as emotion or disposition, it also eliminates any grounds for believing that the spirit is significantly personalized in this text.

The final conclusion is overwhelmingly negative: there is no personalization of the spirit within the limits of the Old Testament.

V. Conclusion

This is the spirit of God, power, anger, life, mind, will, presence, that was manifested in Yahweh's powerful saving act at the Reed

Sea, that was bestowed upon the elders, the judges and the leaders in Israel's early history, that led her in her days of rebellion, that judged and chastised her in the exile, and that finally pointed her to the new age when the hearts of men will be changed by the spirit, and 'justice will dwell in the wilderness, and righteousness abide in the fruitful field, and the effect of righteousness will be peace, and the result of righteousness, quietness and trust forever'.

BIBLIOGRAPHY

A. Books

Alexander, J.A., *Isaiah Translated and Explained* (New York: John Wiley, 1851).

Barnes, W.E., *Haggai and Zechariah* (Cambridge: Cambridge University Press, 1917).

Baumgärtel, F., *Spirit of God* (London: A. and C. Black, 1960).

Brown, Francis, S.R. Driver, and C.A. Briggs, *A Hebrew and English Lexicon of the Old Testament: With an Appendix Containing the Biblical Aramaic: Based on the Lexicon of William Gesenius as Translated by Edward Robinson* (Oxford: Clarendon Press, 1952).

Buber, Martin, *The Prophetic Faith* (New York: Harper and Row, 1949).

Burton, E.D., *Spirit, Soul, and Flesh* (Chicago: University of Chicago Press, 1918).

Briggs, C.A. and E.G. Briggs, *A Critical and Exegetical Commentary on the Book of Psalms* (ICC; Edinburgh: T & T Clark, 1906).

Bright, John, *A History of Israel* (Philadelphia; Westminster, 1959).

Calvin, John, *Commentary on the Four Last Books of Moses* (Grand Rapids: Eerdmans, 1959).

Cassuto, Umberto, *A Commentary on the Book of Genesis* (Jerusalem: Magnes Press, 1961).

Cheyne, T.K., *The Prophecies of Isaiah* (London: C. Kegan Paul, 1880).

Childs, Brevard S., *Myth and Reality in the Old Testament* (London: SCM Press, 1960).

Cooke, C.A., *The Book of Ezekiel* (Cambridge: Cambridge University Press, 1906).

Dalglish, Edward R., *Psalm Fifty-One in the Light of Ancient Near Eastern Patternism* (Leiden: E.J. Brill, 1962).

Delitzsch, Franz, *Biblical Commentary on the Prophecies of Isaiah* (trans. James Martin; Edinburgh: T&T Clark, 1867).

Dentan, R.C., *I and II Kings, I and II Chronicles* (London: SCM Press, 1964).

Driver, G.R., *Canaanite Myths and Legends* (Edinburgh: T&T Clark, 1956).

Driver, S.R., *An Introduction to the Literature of the Old Testament* (New York: Meridian Library 1956).

—*Joel and Amos* (Cambridge: Cambridge University Press, 1915).

Driver, Samuel H., *Notes on the Hebrew Text of Samuel* (Oxford: Clarendon, 1913).

Eerdmans, B.D., *The Hebrew Book of Psalms* (Leiden: E.J. Brill, 1947).

Eichrodt, W., *Der Prophet Hesekiel, Kapitel 1-18* (ATD; Göttingen: Vandenhoeck und Ruprecht, 1959).

—*Theology of the Old Testament* (2 vols.; London: SCM Press, 1961).

Elliger, K., *Das Buch der zwölf kleinen Propheten* (ATD, Göttingen: Vandenhoeck und Ruprecht, 1951).

Elmslie, W.A.L., *Chronicles,* in G.A. Buttrick (ed.), The Interpreter's Bible (New York: Abingdon-Cokesbury Press, 1951).

Fohrer, G., *Das Buch Jesaja* (Zürich: Zwingli Verlag, 1962).

— *Überlieferung und Geschichte des Exodus* (Berlin: Alfred Töpelmann, 1964).

Galling, Kurt, *Die Bücher der Chronik* (ATD; Göttingen: Vandenhoeck und Ruprecht, 1954).

Gray, G.B., *The Book of Isaiah* (New York: Charles Scribner's Sons, 1912).

Gunkel, Hermann, *Die Wirkungen des heiligen Geistes* (Göttingen: Vandenhoeck und Ruprecht, 1888).

Herntrich, Volkmar, *Der Prophet Jesaja* (ATD, Göttingen: Vandenhoeck und Ruprecht, 1950).

Horst F., *Hiob* (BK, Neukirchen: Neukirchener Verlag, 1960).

—*Nahum bis Maleachi* (Tübingen: J.C.B. Mohr, 1954).

Hölscher, Gustav, *Das Buch Hiob* (Handbuch zum Alten Testament; Tübingen: J.C.B. Mohr (P. Siebeck), 1952).

Jeffery, Arthur, *The Book of Daniel,* in G.A. Buttrick (ed.), The Interpreter's Bible (New York: Abingdon-Cokesbury Press, 1951).

Jepsen, Alfred, *Nabi* (München: C.H. Beck, 1934).

Johnson, Aubrey R., *The Cultic Prophet in Ancient Israel* (Cardiff: Univsersity of Wales Press, 1962).

Kapelrud, A.S., *Joel Studies* (Uppsala: Almqvist Wiksells, 1948).

Gesenius, Wilhelm, E. Kautzsch, and A.E. Cowley, *Gesenius' Hebrew Grammar* (Oxford: The Clarendon Press, 2d English edn, 1910).

Keil, C.F., *Prophecies of Ezekiel* (Grand Rapids: Eerdmans, 1949).

—*The Twelve Minor Prophets* (Grand Rapids: Eerdmans 1949).

Koch, Robert, *Geist und Messias* (Wien: Verlag Herder, 1950).

Kraus, H.J., *Psalmen* (Neukirchen: Neukirchener Verlag, 1960).

Leslie, Elmer, *Isaiah* (Nashville: Abingdon, 1963).

Lindblom, J., *Prophecy in Ancient Israel* (Philadelphia, Fortress Press, 1962).

—'Wisdom in the Old Testament Prophets', in M. Noth and D. Winton Thomas (eds.), *Wisdom in Israel and in The Ancient Near East* (Leiden: E.J. Brill, 1955).

Linder, Sven, *Studier till Gamla Testamentets Föreställningar Om Anden* (Uppsala: Almqvist and Wiksell, 1926).

Lys, Daniel, *Ruach, le Souffle dans l'Ancien Testament* (Paris: Presses Universitaires de France, 1962).

Maertens, Thierry, *Le Souffle et l'Esprit de Dieu* (Bruges: Desclee De Brouwer, 1959).

Mauchline, John, *Isaiah 1-39* (London: SCM Press, 1962).

May, Herbert G., *Ezekiel,* in G.A. Buttrick (ed.), The Interpreter's Bible (New York: Abingdon-Cokesbury Press, 1951).

McKane, W., *Prophets and Wise Men* (London: SCM Press, 1965).

Montgomery, J.A., *The Book of Daniel* (NY: Charles Scribner's Sons, 1927).

Muilenburg, James, *Isaiah,* in G.A. Buttrick (ed.), The Interpreter's Bible (New York: Abingdon-Cokesbury Press, 1956).

Myers, Jacob M., *1 Chronicles* (AB; Garden City: Doubleday, 1965).

Néher, André, *L'Essence du Prophétisme* (Paris: Presses Universitaires de France, 1955).

Noth, Martin, *Exodus* (London: SCM Press, 1962).

Porteous, Norman, *Daniel* (Philadelphia, Westminster, 1965).

Rad, Gerhard von, 'Die levitische Predigt in den Büchern der Chronik', in Albrecht Alt (ed.), *Festschrift Otto Procksch zum sechzigsten Geburtstag* (Leipzig: Deichert, 1934), pp. 113-24.

—*Genesis,* (London, SCM Press).

—*Gesammelte Studien* (München: C. Kaiser, 1958).

—*Old Testament Theology* (2 vols.; London: Oliver & Boyd, 1962).

Ridderbos, Nic. H., 'Genesis 1.1 und 2', in P.A.H. De Boer (ed.), *Oudtestamentische Studien* (Leiden: E.J. Brill, 1958).

Robinson, H. Wheeler, 'Hebrew Psychology', in A.S. Peake (ed.), *The People and the Book* (Oxford: Clarendon Press, 1925), pp. 353-382.

Scheepers, Johannes H., *Die Gees van God en die Gees van die mens in die Oud Testament* (Kampen : J.H. Kok, 1960).

Schmidt, Werner H., *Die Schöpfungsgeschichte der Priesterschrift* (Neukirchen: Neukirchener Verlag, 1964).

Sethe, Kurt, *Amun und die acht Urgötter von Hermopolis* (Berlin: Verlag der Akademie der Wissenschaften, 1929).

Simpson, C.A., *The Book of Genesis,* in G.A. Buttrick (ed.), The Interpreter's Bible (New York: Abingdon-Cokesbury Press, 1951).

Skinner, John, *A Critical and Exegetical Commentary on Genesis* (ICC; New York: Charles Scribner's Sons, 1917).

—*Isaiah* (Cambridge: Cambridge University Press, 1922).

Smart, J., *History and Theology in Second Isaiah* (Philadelphia: Westminster 1965).

Snaith, Norman, *Amos, Hosea, and Micah* (London: Epworth, 1956).

—*Distinctive Ideas of the Old Testament* (London: Epworth, 1944).

—*The First and Second Books of Kings,* in G.A. Buttrick (ed.), The Interpreter's Bible (New York: Abingdon-Cokesbury Press, 1951).

Speiser, E.A., *Genesis* (AB; Garden City: Doubleday, 1964).

Terrien, Samuel, *Job* (Neuchâtel: Delachaux and Niestlé, 1963).

—*Job,* in G.A. Buttrick (ed.), The Interpreter's Bible (New York: Abingdon-Cokesbury Press, 1951).

Thompson, J.A., *Joel,* in G.A. Buttrick (ed.), The Interpreter's Bible (New York: Abingdon-Cokesbury Press, 1951).

Tur-Sinai, N.H., *The Book of Job: A New Commentary* (Jerusalem: Kiryath Sepher, 1957).

Volz, Paul, *Der Geist Gottes* (Tübingen: J.C.B. Mohr, 1910).

Weiser, Artur, *Introduction to the Old Testament* (trans. Dorothea M. Barton; London: Darton, Longman & Todd, 1961).

—*The Psalms* (London: SCM Press, 1962).

Welch, Adam C., *The Work of the Chronicler* (London: Oxford Press, 1939).

Wolfe, Roland, *Micah,* in G.A. Buttrick (ed.), The Interpreter's Bible (New York: Abingdon-Cokesbury Press, 1951).

Wolff, H.W., *Joel* (BK, Neukirchen: Neukirchener Verlag, 1963).

Wood, Irving F., *The Spirit of God in Biblical Literature* (New York: A.C. Armstrong, 1904).

Zimmerli, Walther, *Ezechiel* (BK; Neukirchen: Neukirchener Verlag, 1969).

B. Periodicals

Albright, W.F., 'Zabul Yam and Thapit Nahar in the Combat between Baal and the Sea', *Journal of the Palestine Oriental Society* 16 (1936), pp. 17-20.

Armerding, C., 'The Holy Spirit in the Old Testament', *Bibliotheca Sacra* 92 (1935), pp. 277-91, 433-41.

Blythin, I., 'A Note on Genesis 1, 2', *Vetus Testamentum* 12 (1962), pp. 120-21.

Briggs, C.A., 'The use of רוח in the Old Testament', *Journal of Biblical Literature* 19 (1900), pp. 132-45.

Caspari, Wilhelm, 'Der Geist des Herrn ist über mir', *Neue Kirchliche Zeitschrift* 13 (1902), pp. 321-47, 403-427.

Cripps, P.S., 'The Holy Spirit in the Old Testament', *Theology* 24 (1932), pp. 272-80.

Cross, Frank M., Jr. and David Noel Freedman, 'The Song of Miriam', *JNES* 14 (1955), pp. 239-50.

Dussaud, Rene, 'La néphesh et la rouah dans le "Livre de Job"', *Revue de l'Histoire des Religions* 129 (1945), pp. 17-30.

—'Les trois premiers versets de la Genese', *Revue de l'Histoire des Religions* Tome C (1929), pp. 137-39.

Galling, Kurt, 'Der Charakter der Chaosschilderung in Genesis 1, 2', *Zeitschrift für Theologie und Kirche* 47 (1950), pp. 145-57.

Hehn, J., 'Zum Problem des Geistes im alten Orient und im AT', *Zeitschrift für die Alttestamentliche Wissenschaft* 43 (1925), pp. 218-25.

Hummel, H., 'Enclitic *mem* in Early Northwest Semitic, Especially Hebrew', *Journal of Biblical Literature* 76 (1957), pp. 85-107.

Imschoot, P. van, 'L'Action de l'Esprit de Jahvé dans l'AT', *Revue des Sciences Philosophiques et Theologiques* 23 (1934), pp. 553-87.

—'L'Esprit de Jahvé et l' alliance nouvelle dans l'AT', *Ephemerides Theologicae Lovanienses* 13 (1936), pp. 201-220.

—'L'Esprit de Jahvé, principe de vie morale dans l'AT', *Ephemerides Theologicae Lovanienses* 16 (1939), pp. 457-67.

—'L'Esprit de Jahvé, source de la piéte dans l'AT', *Bible et Vie Chretienne* 6 (1954), pp. 17-30.

—'L'Esprit de Jahvé, source de vie dans l'AT', *Revue Biblique* 44 (1935), pp. 481-501.

—'Sagesse et Esprit dans l'AT', *Revue Biblique* 47 (1938), pp. 23-49.

Joüon, Paul, 'Quelques remarques sur Gen. 1:2', *Recherches de Science Religieuse* 16 (1926), pp. 304-307.

Kilian, R., 'Gen. 1, 2 und die Urgötter von Hermopolis', *Vetus Testamentum* 16 (1966), pp. 420-38.

Köberle, Justin, 'Gottesgeist und Menschengeist im AT', *Neue Kirchliche Zeitschrift* 13 (1902), pp. 321-47, 403-427.

May, H., 'The Creation of Light in Genesis 1.3-5', *Journal of Biblical Literature* 43 (1939).

McClellan, William, 'The Meaning of rûach 'Elohim in Genesis 1, 2' *Biblica* 15 (1934), pp. 517-27.

Moscati, Sabatino, 'The Wind in Biblical and Phoenician Cosmogony', *Journal of Biblical Literature* 56 (1947), pp. 305-310.

Mowinckel, Sigmund, 'The "Spirit" and the "Word" in the Pre-exilic Reforming Prophets', *Journal of Biblical Literature* 53 (1934), pp. 199-227; 56 (1937), pp. 261-65.

Muilenburg, James, 'The Literary Character of Isaiah 34', *Journal of Biblical Literature* 59.3 (1940), pp. 339-65.

North, C.R., 'The Religious Aspects of Hebrew Kingship', *ZAW* 50 (1932), pp. 8-38.

Orlinsky, Harry, 'The Plain Meaning of Ruach in Gen. 1:2', *The Jewish Quarterly Review* 48 (1957/8), pp. 174-82.

Peters, J.P., 'The Wind of God', *Journal of Biblical Literature* 30 (1911), pp. 44-54; 33 (1914), pp. 81-86.

Procksch, Otto, 'Die letzten Worte Davids', *Beiträge zur Wissenschaft vom Alten Testament* 13 (1913), pp. 112-25.

Schoemaker, W.R., 'The Use of רוח in the Old Testament and πνεῦμα in the New Testament', *Journal of Biblical Literature* 23 (1904), pp. 13-67.

Smith, J.M.P., 'The Syntax and Meaning of Genesis 1.1-3', *American Journal of Semitic Languages* 44 (1927-8), pp. 111-14; 45 (1928-29), pp. 212-13.

—'The Use of Divine Names as Superlatives', *American Journal of Semitic Languages and Literatures* 45 (1928-29), pp. 212-13.

Smoronski, K., 'Et spiritus Dei ferebatur super aquas', *Biblica* 6 (1925), pp. 140-56, 275-93, 361-95.

Thomas, D. Winton, 'A Consideration of Some Unusual Ways of Expressing the Superlative in Hebrew', *Vetus Testamentum* 3 (1953), pp. 209-24.

Waterman, L., 'Cosmogonic Affinities in Genesis 1.2', *American Journal of Semitic Literature* 43 (1927), pp. 177-84.

Weinel, H., 'משח und seine Derivate', *Zeitschrift für die Alttestamentliche Wissenschaft* 18 (1898), pp. 55-56.

Young, Edward J., 'The Interpretation of Genesis 1.2', *Westminster Theological Journal* 23 (1960-1961), pp. 151-78.

C. Unpublished Materials

Terrien, Samuel, 'Old Testament Theology' (New York: Union Theological Seminary, unpublished classroom lectures).

Westphal, Mylio, 'La Ruach dans l'Ancien Testament'. Bachelor of Theology dissertation (The University of Geneva, Geneva, 1958).

APPENDIX

Biblical Texts Using Ruach as Wind

Genesis
3.8
8.1

Exodus
10.13, 19
14.21

Numbers
11.312

I Samuel
22.11

1 Kings
18.45
19.11

2 Kings
3.17

Isaiah
7.2
17.13
26.18
27.8
32.2
40.7
41.16, 29
57.13
59.19
64.5

Jeremiah
2.24
4.11, 12
5.13
10.13

13.24
14.6
18.17
22.22
49.32, 36
51.1, 16
52.23

Ezekiel
1.4
5.2, 10, 12
12.14
13.11, 13
17.10, 21
19.12
27.26
37.9
42.16, 17, 18, 19, 20

Hosea
4.19
8.7
12.2
13.15

Amos
4.13

Jonah
1.4
4.8

Micah
2.11

Habakkuk
1.11

Zechariah
2.10
5.9
6.5

Psalms
1.4
11.6
18.11, 43
35.5
48.8
55.9
83.14
103.16
104.3, 4
107.25
135.7
148.8

Job
1.19
4.15
6.26
8.2
15.2, 30
16.3
21.18
28.25
30.15, 22
37.21
41.8

Proverbs
11.29
25.14, 23

27.16
30.4

Ecclesiastes
1.6, 14, 17
2.11, 17, 26
4.4, 6, 16
5.15
6.9
11.4, 5

Daniel
2.35
7.2
8.8
11.4

1 Chronicles
9.24

Biblical Texts Using Ruach as the Human Spirit

Genesis
  6.3, 17
  7.15, 22
  26.35
  41.8
  45.27

Exodus
  6.9
  35.21

Numbers
  5.14, 30
  14.24
  16.22
  27.16

Deuteronomy
  2.30

Joshua
  2.11
  5.1

Judges
  8.3
  15.19

1 Samuel
  1.15
  30.12

1 Kings
  10.5
  21.5

2 Kings
  2.9, 15

Isaiah
  11.4
  19.3, 14
  25.4
  26.9

  28.6
  29.10, 24
  33.11
  38.16
  42.5
  54.6
  57.15, 16
  61.3
  65.14
  66.2

Jeremiah
  10.14
  51.11, 17

Ezekiel
  3.14
  11.5, 19
  13.3
  18.31
  20.32
  21.12
  36.26
  37.5, 6, 8, 9, 10

Hosea
  4.12
  5.4

Habakkuk
  2.19

Haggai
  1.14

Zechariah
  12.1, 10

Malachi
  2.15, 16

Psalms
  31.6

  32.2
  34.19
  51.12, 14, 19
  76.13
  77.4, 7
  78.8, 39
  104.29
  106.33
  135.17
  142.4
  143.4, 7
  146.4

Job
  6.4
  7.7, 11
  9.18
  10.12
  12.10
  15.13
  17.1
  19.17
  20.3
  21.4
  27.3
  32.18

Proverbs
  1.23
  11.13
  14.29
  15.4, 13
  16.2, 18, 19, 32
  17.22, 27
  18.14
  25.28
  29.11, 23

Ecclesiastes
  3.19, 21
  7.8, 9

8.8
10.4
12.7

Lamentations
4.2

Daniel
2.1, 3
5.12, 20
6.4
7.15

Ezra
1.1, 5

1 Chronicles
5.26
28.12

2 Chronicles
9.4
21.16
36.22

Biblical Texts Using Ruach as an Evil Spirit

Judges
  9.23

1 Samuel
  16.14, 15, 16
  18.10
  19.9

1 Kings
  22.21, 22, 23

2 Kings
  19.7

Isaiah
  37.7

Zechariah
  13.2

2 Chronicles
  18.20, 21, 22

Index of Biblical Texts Using Ruach as the Spirit of God

Other Books from CPT Press

www.cptpress.com

R. Hollis Gause, *Living in the Spirit: The Way of Salvation* (2009). ISBN 9780981965109

Kenneth J. Archer, *A Pentecostal Hermeneutic: Spirit, Scripture and Community* (2009). ISBN 9780981965116

Larry McQueen, *Joel and the Spirit: The Cry of a Prophetic Hermeneutic* (2009). ISBN 9780981965123

Lee Roy Martin, *Introduction to Biblical Hebrew* (2009). ISBN 9780981965154

Lee Roy Martin, *Answer Key to Introduction to Biblical Hebrew* (2009). ISBN 9780981965161

Lee Roy Martin, *Workbook for Introduction to Biblical Hebrew* (2010). ISBN 9780981965185

Martin William Mittelstadt, *Reading Luke–Acts in the Pentecostal Tradition* (2010). ISBN 9780981965178

Roger Stronstad, *The Prophethood of All Believers* (2010). ISBN 9780981965130

Kristen Dayle Welch, *'Women with the Good News': The Rhetorical Heritage of Pentecostal Holiness Women Preachers* (2010). ISBN 9780981965192

Steven Jack Land, *Pentecostal Spirituality: A Passion for the Kingdom* (2010). ISBN 9780981965147

John Christopher Thomas (ed.), *Toward a Pentecostal Ecclesiology: The Church and the Fivefold Gospel* (2010). ISBN 9781935931003

Robert P. Menzies, *The Language of the Spirit: Interpreting and Translating Charismatic Terms* (2010). ISBN 9781935931010

John Christopher Thomas, *The Devil, Disease, and Deliverance: Origins of Healing in New Testament Thought* (2011). ISBN 9781935931034

Larry R. McQueen, *Toward a Pentecostal Eschatology: Discerning the Way Forward* (2011). ISBN 9781935931157

Margaret Gaines, *Small Enough to Stop the Violence?: Arabs, Christians, and Jews* (2011). ISBN 9781935931188

Many of these books are available for the iPad and Kindle.

www.ingramcontent.com/pod-product-compliance
Lightning Source LLC
Chambersburg PA
CBHW071349090426
42738CB00012B/3062